W9-APD-332

The
Elgin, Joliet and Eastern
Railway

THE
ELGIN, JOLIET AND EASTERN RAILWAY

Patrick C. Dorin

AROUND – NOT THRU CHICAGO

SIGNATURE PRESS

Berkeley and Wilton, California

The Elgin, Joliet and Eastern Railway

Copyright © 2009 by Patrick C. Dorin

All rights reserved. No part of this publication may be reproduced or distributed in any form or by any means, including photocopy, nor may it be stored in a database or retrieval system, without the prior written permission of the publisher.

Published by Signature Press
11508 Green Road
Wilton, CA 95693
www.signaturepress.com

Publisher's Cataloging-in-Publication
(Provided by Quality Books, Inc.)

    Dorin, Patrick C.
      The Elgin, Joliet and Eastern railway : around, not
   thru Chicago / Patrick C. Dorin.
      p. cm.
      Includes bibliographical references and index.
      LCCN 2009934093
      ISBN-13: 9781930013261
      ISBN-10: 1930013264

      1. Elgin, Joliet and Eastern Railway--History.
   2. Railroads--United States--History. 3. Railroads--
   Illinois--Chicago--History.   I. Title.

    TF25.E44D67 2009   385'.0973
                       QBI09-600139

Frontispiece and dust jacket: this watercolor depicts an EJ&E freight train powered by a distinctive Baldwin center-cab locomotive, passing the Griffith, Indiana depot, and is based on a Russ Porter photograph.

Book design and typography by Lori Daniel

Printed in China

Dedicated To

Clinton Ferner, Former Superintendent for The Elgin, Joliet and Eastern Railway
And
General Manager for the Duluth, Missabe & Iron Range Railway

Clint Ferner is a delightful person to work for and with. This writer had an opportunity to work with Clint on the EJ&E. He has a strong and a broad knowledge base of railroad operations and marketing for shippers. Clint is serving on the Lake Superior Railroad Museum Board of Directors

ACKNOWLEDGMENTS

Many people contributed ideas, suggestions, photographs, and provided the author with time and the opportunities for research for this book on the Elgin, Joliet and Eastern Railway. People from the EJ&E include John Pranaitis, M.S. Turner, Clinton Ferner, Ken Hay, James Jamrus, Carl Harton, Gerald Carr, Jon Hankins, John Murray and Pam Murrow. and Joe Wojcik.

Rail photographers and photo collectors include Russ Porter, Jim Scribbins, Frank Schnick, Tom Dorin, Harold Vollrath, William Kuba, William Raia, Terry Hand, Jay Williams, Alan Turner, Dan Mackey, Tom Klinger, Bob's Photo, Bill Sheehan, Richard Buike, David Schauer, Ed Kaminski, and J. Michael Gruber. Permission to to use the drawings of business car No. 40 was granted by Carstens Publications. Freight car photos (and photo permissions) and information, as well as assistance with the freight car chapters, was kindly provided by Richard Hendrickson and Anthony Thompson. Color maps were prepared by John R. Signor from original materials provided by EJ&E.

Without the kind assistance of these people, the book on the EJ&E would not have been possible. Thank you each and every one for your time, wisdom, photographic skills and keeping "track" of the history of the EJ&E.

Contents

INTRODUCTION

The Elgin, Joliet and Eastern Railway, commonly known as "The J" has been serving the Chicago area and the steel industry since the late 1880s. The railroad has provided a base line for transportation services for U.S. Steel and other companies as well for interchange traffic on the "Around – Not Thru Chicago" main line between Waukegan and Gary and Porter, Indiana.

The book takes a quick look into the history of the railroad and then covers the types of train services since the 1940s to the present time. Motive power and freight equipment are a crucial part of such services, for without the "Tools of the Trade," no service could be provided in any way, shape or form. The EJ&E provided a highly reliable freight service, which is extremely important for shippers. The types of services have also changed over the years including new levels of trackage and haulage rights over the main lines as we move deeper into the 21st century.

The J was one of the first railroads to be 100% dieselized by 1948. The company had operated a variety of modern steam power, and then dived into the road-switcher concept ahead of most other rail carriers. This type of power was most appropriate for the J because of the variety of switching that needed to be done at the many interchange points as well as yard work.

The J has also had some interesting color schemes over the years with a combination of orange and green for the motive power, and then all orange; and the same held true for a variety of freight equipment. This was particularly true for box cars. The company owned and operated a wide variety of equipment. Rosters from different time periods are included for the purpose of assisting the artistic model railroaders who are modeling various periods of operations on the EJ&E.

The EJ&E continues to play an important role with its geographic locations around Chicago. It has the ability to save an enormous amount of time for freight shipments between the eastern and western carriers. One could say it is the cornerstone for many of train operations and services provided by Class I railroads. Indeed, because of its geographic location, the railroad may soon be operating commuter passenger services "Around – Not Thru Chicago." This is currently happening in California, a state that *now* (2004) has more passenger trains than it has had over the last 75 years — or even for its entire history. But that is another story. It is very interesting that the EJ&E could soon playing an even bigger role for transportation in the Chicago Area.

This book was completed in 2004. There were a few changes in operation from 2005 to 2008, and then in early 2009 the EJ&E was purchased by Canadian National. Operations described here as "at the present time" reflect the 2004–2005 period.

Patrick C. Dorin
Superior, Wisconsin
July 30, 2009

- PART I -

TRAIN OPERATIONS AND SERVICE

The first six chapters of this book on the EJ&E review the types of train services and operations provided by the company for many industries, and for the interchange service between railroads around Chicago. The company's slogan:

"Around – Not Thru Chicago"

tells exactly what the Elgin, Joliet and Eastern Railway really is. Its strategic geographic location provides the answer to many of the congestion problems for moving freight through Chicagoland. In fact, Belt Line operations are also beginning for commuter rail passenger services at localities such as Los Angeles and the San Francisco Bay area. One such plan is also being studied in the Chicago area which would involve the EJ&E. It would add a new dimension to the company's slogan.

Early motive power on the EJ&E and its predecessors included the various types found on many railroads in the 1890s and early 1900s. EJ&E No. 41, a 4-4-0, was built by Rhode Island in 1892. Its portrait was taken in South Chicago about 1900.

(Harold K. Vollrath collection)

Chapter 1

AROUND – NOT THRU CHICAGO: A BIT OF HISTORY

A Bit of History

THE Elgin, Joliet and Eastern Railway was incorporated in the year 1888. The company was the result of several mergers into or with the parent corporate company with a rather interesting ancestral history. An authoritative book, written by A.M. Auffart and published by the EJ&E in 1988, entitled *The Elgin, Joliet and Eastern Railway Company, A History of the Early Development of a Regional Railroad*, describes in detail the development of this railroad, which eventually became a subsidiary of U.S. Steel.

Let's take a quick look at the development of "The J" from the very first idea for the railroad, which literally rolls back to the year 1881. Plans were made for building a railroad known as the LaPorte and Illinois Railroad to join still another line known as the Joliet and Indiana Railroad. The two companies consolidated to create new company known as the Joliet, Indiana and Eastern Railway, which by the way, never so much as laid a rail or even a tie.

The next step took place in 1884 when the Joliet, Aurora and Northern Railway was incorporated. Construction began in 1886, and the first train between Joliet and Aurora ran on August 15, 1886. Part of the train services included a twice daily passenger train operation between Joliet and Aurora, which was eventually discontinued in 1907. Electric interurban trains were providing a more frequent service with more station stops.

The year 1887 is an important year in the history of the EJ&E. The Elgin, Joliet and Eastern Railway of Illinois was incorporated on March 18, 1887. The plan was to build the railroad from Spaulding, Illinois to Valparaiso, Indiana. Less than a month later, in order to

accomplish this objective, the Elgin, Joliet and Eastern Railway of Indiana was incorporated on April 13, 1887. The framework was beginning to come together, but there is more to the story, which takes the J on some rather interesting twists and turns.

Early in 1888, plans for a coal line were created with the route from Gardner, Illinois northward to tie in with the Joliet, Aurora and Northern at Plainfield, Illinois, which is about 7 miles north of East Joliet on the J's Western Subdivision. The coal line was incorporated as the Gardner, Coal City and Northern Railway in May, 1888. That same year, main line construction reached the Chicago & North Western Railway and the "St. Paul Road," later to be known as the Milwaukee Road. And to make things even more interesting, construction of a rail line to an eastern terminal at Porter, Indiana was under serious consideration.

Getting back to the coal line, trackage reached Gardner in August, 1888. At that time, 40 carloads of coal were moving north on a daily basis from Braidwood Mines to Spaulding, Illinois. As the year 1888 continued, the Joliet, Aurora and Northern was merged into the EJ&E of Illinois. In December of that year, the EJ&E of Illinois and the EJ&E of Indiana were consolidated into the Elgin, Joliet and Eastern Railway Company. The red number date of importance was December 4th. And new developments were already underway.

One of the new ideas in 1888 was extending the railroad from Spaulding to Waukegan, Illinois. And jumping into early 1889, the Gardner, Coal City and Northern Railway was leased to the EJ&E.

The year 1889 say the incorporation of the Waukegan and Southwestern Railway. Construction started right away and the railroad reached the Wisconsin Central

Ten-Wheelers were also on board early in the EJ&E's history. No. 62 was built by Baldwin in 1898 as No. 32 and it proudly displays the insignia "Chicago Outer Belt Line" on the tender. This was the only Vauclain compound on the EJ&E, and its photo was taken about 1900, the same time the image on page 10 of No. 41 in South Chicago. *(Harold K. Vollrath collection)*

This photo of the small depot at Minooka, Illinois dates from the 1890s. *(Richard Buike collection)*

Railway in August at Leithton. Waukegan was reached in early 1890. The next corporate step took place immediately with the EJ&E leasing the Waukegan and Southwestern Railway.

The corporate structure was really rolling along, full steam ahead. The year 1891 saw the Gardner, Coal City and Northern and the Waukegan and Southwestern folded into the EJ&E. The EJ&E was growing with 166 miles of main line and yard trackage with 31 locomotives and 1075 freight cars with a few passenger cars as part of the roster. The J handled 1.5 million tons of freight in 1891. Things were going quite well.

The extension to Porter, Indiana was completed in 1893, and was officially opened on June 22nd of that year. Meanwhile, the roster had grown to 42 locomotives and 2600 freight cars. Trains and new ideas continued to roll for the EJ&E. The year 1897 saw the incorporation of the Chicago Heights and Northern Railway. The purpose was to build a railroad line into South Chicago. At the same time, a railroad known as the Western Indiana was purchased. This line was originally designated to be built from Hammond, Indiana to LaPorte. However, only 1 mile of line was ever built between the State Line at Hammond and the Corning steel mill.

Once the Western Indiana was within the EJ&E fold, the line was extended from Corning to Shearson and then north to the Standard Oil Refinery in Whiting, Indiana. The construction was completed in early 1897. The Western Indiana, and the Chicago Heights and Northern, were consolidated as the Chicago Heights and Northern in 1897. Two years later in 1899, the CH&N was folded into the EJ&E.

The coal line branch was extended one more mile further south to South Wilmington for additional access to the coal fields in 1899. Meanwhile, throughout the 1890s, other bits of history and development were taking place that would soon have an impact of the expansion and development of the Elgin, Joliet and Eastern Railway.

The Calumet and Blue Island Railroad obtained a trackage rights agreement with the Chicago and Eastern Illinois Railroad in 1893. This route extended into Southern Illinois and into Indiana tapping coal fields as well as limestone. The agreement was that the C&BI could handle only coal loads and limestone northbound, and empties only southbound. The C&BI was consolidated into the Chicago, Lake Shore and Eastern Railway in 1897, still another railroad company to become part of the EJ&E. In fact, the CLS&E was using a portion of the EJ&E for its coal traffic over the C&EI. This was an important source of traffic flow because the Illinois Steel Company purchased the EJ&E in 1898.

Many of the EJ&E station and track side buildings were light gray. Without a significant passenger service, the stations served as train order offices including facilities for freight. One example is the freight house shown here at Barrington, Illinois. Other Maintenance of Way buildings and facilities are at the right of the photo. Many of the stations also included an agent for the freight services. This photo at Barrington was taken in June, 1977. Barrington was (is) an interchange connection with the Chicago and North Western, now Union Pacific. It would also be a station stop for Metra commuter train services when that plan goes into action sometime in, hopefully, the near future; please refer to Chapter 6. *(Harold K. Vollrath collection)*

Later in 1898, Illinois Steel Company was merged into the Federal Steel Company, a combine organized by J.P. Morgan; three years later, Federal merged with America's largest steelmaker, Carnegie Steel, and eight other companies to form United States Steel. This meant that the EJ&E became a subsidiary of U.S. Steel as part of the heritage from Illinois Steel.

As it moved into the twentieth century, the EJ&E owned and operated 56 steam locomotives, 2073 cars including three passenger cars. The sister railroad, the CLS&E operated 62 locomotives with 4,384 freight cars. A new branch line for the EJ&E was incorporated in April, 1904 as the Rockdale, Joliet and Lockport Terminal Railroad. The line was officially purchased in 1905.

The year 1905 was another big year for the EJ&E. U.S. Steel began construction of new steel mill in Gary, Indiana. The CLS&E was to do the switching. The EJ&E officially purchased the Chicago, Lake Shore and Eastern in 1909. Part of the original trackage of the CLS&E extended between Indiana Harbor and Clark Road in Gary was abandoned in 1911. Operations of both railroads were more fully integrated from that time on. The CLS&E was officially merged into the EJ&E in December, 1938.

The EJ&E's operations over the Chicago and Eastern Illinois were given up in 1948. Still other trackage cut backs would take place in the 1970s and 80s. For example, the Aurora branch was cut back around 1975 and completely abandoned in 1985. The Porter branch from Griffith, Indiana to Porter was also abandoned in 1985. Operations into South Chicago from the Hammond area were also discontinued. However, the EJ&E still operates into South Chicago along the Lake Front line.

So What Did the EJ&E Map Look Like Since the 1950s?

The railroad, although known now for many years as "The J," was also known as the "Chicago Outer Belt," which is still an appropriate name. In fact, it may become an even more important concept in the years to come as various traffic patterns change between the eastern and western carriers converging on the Chicago area.

The J's main line consists of a belt line encircling the City of Chicago at a distance of 30 to 40 miles from the downtown area known as the Loop. The EJ&E extends from Waukegan, Illinois (36 miles north of Chicago) and to Joliet, Illinois. At Joliet, the trackage turns eastward toward Chicago Heights and Griffith, Indiana. At that point, the line once split with one segment heading east to Porter, Indiana. The other route headed in a northerly

direction toward Gary, Indiana. On the far west side of Gary, the line turned eastward toward Kirk Yard and the gigantic Gary Works of U.S. Steel.

The EJ&E literally intersects every railroad entering Chicago, even with the abandonment of the Porter line. Routes also extend westward from Gary toward South Chicago and the Hammond, Whiting and East Chicago area. The company serves many industries in this Southeast "South Chicago–Gary" geographical area.

For a very brief period of time during the spring of 1980, the EJ&E had trackage rights over the Rock Island Railroad from Joliet to Peoria. One of the objectives of the operation was to enable The J to add another facet for the company's freight traffic. However, The J was not a successful bidder in acquiring this line from the Rock Island's bankruptcy trustee.

The company had been owned by U.S. Steel Corporation between 1899 and 1988. In 1988, the U.S. Steel transportation companies, including the EJ&E, were sold to a partnership of U.S. Steel and Blackstone Group called "Transtar." In 2000, the Transtar properties were split, with the Duluth, Missabe & Iron Range, the Bessemer & Lake Erie, and the Great Lakes fleet of ships being wholly acquired by Blackstone, while the EJ&E, the Union Railroad, Birmingham Southern and other properties and operations returned to the U.S. Steel fold.

It was an interesting period of time when the EJ&E was part of a full family of railroads such as the DM&IR and the B&LE. Many locomotives and pieces of rolling stock were sold or traded among these railroads over the years. One example was various steam locomotives from the EJ&E and the B&LE which went to the DM&IR. Another colorful example from the 2004 period is that a number of locomotives on the EJ&E still carried the DM&IR colors but with EJ&E lettering and insignia, as shown in Chapter 8.

The EJ&E continues to play a major role for the steel industry as well as interchange traffic on the intersecting routes around Chicago. As of 2004, EJ&E is still living up to its original corporate plans and ambition—and doing as big a job as ever. [Its sale to Canadian National in 2009 is not discussed in this book.] The remainder of the book has to do with train operations as well as the motive power and rolling stock.

⌒

Before finishing this chapter, speaking of the J as being part of the picture intersecting the various railroad lines in Chicago, it could well be playing a role in commuter train services around Chicago as it intersects the various commuter rail routes. Such a plan is already in effect in Los Angeles and the EJ&E has the most strategic route through a highly populated area that keeps growing.

Maps on the following pages of various stages of growth of the EJ&E are redrawn from maps in the book *The Elgin, Joliet and Eastern Railway Company, A History of the Early Development of a Regional Railroad*, by A. M. Auffart, which was published by the EJ&E in 1988. ❏

Railroad trackage is the baseline foundation for service and operations. This view is looking south geographically, and eastward railroad direction at the Western Subdivision in Centralized Traffic Control territory just north of Joliet. The Western Sub extends from Joliet to Waukegan. The photo was taken on an incredibly beautiful autumn day in October, 2003.

(Patrick C. Dorin)

North Chicago and Waukegan are at the northern end of the Western Subdivision between Joliet and Waukegan. This 1968 photo shows part of the North Chicago and Waukegan yard area with two rebuilt Baldwin Center Cabs laying over between runs between East Joliet Yard and Waukegan.

(Russ Porter)

Freight cars of the EJ&E went everywhere in the country, as would be expected for free-running cars like box cars, and these two photos illustrate the point. The EJ&E had received 500 box cars from the United States Railway Administration (USRA) in 1919, and like many owners of these cars, rebuilt them in later years with new steel sides and doors. They kept their original car numbers in the 7300–7799 series. EJ&E 7727 was photographed in Rocky Mount, North Carolina on December 28, 1951.

(Chet McCoid photo, Bob's Photo collection)

In the 1950s, EJ&E adopted a dramatic paint scheme for its box cars, with the upper part of the car having dark green lettering on an orange background, and the lower part of the car having those colors reversed. EJ&E 60932 was one of 500 cars delivered in 1948 with 8-foot wide Superior doors and 12 side panels. This photo shows a car repainted from the rather plain scheme in which the cars were delivered, and was taken at Zanesville, Ohio on May 15, 1958. *(Paul Dunn photo, J. Michael Gruber collection)*

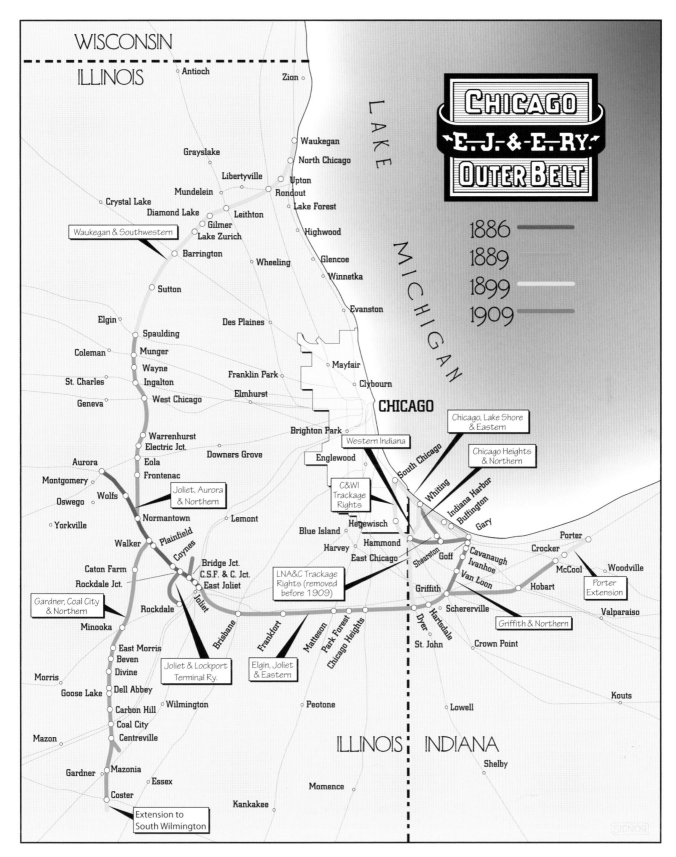

Development of the EJ&E lines up to 1909, with predecessor and intermediate railroad names shown. For details, see text.

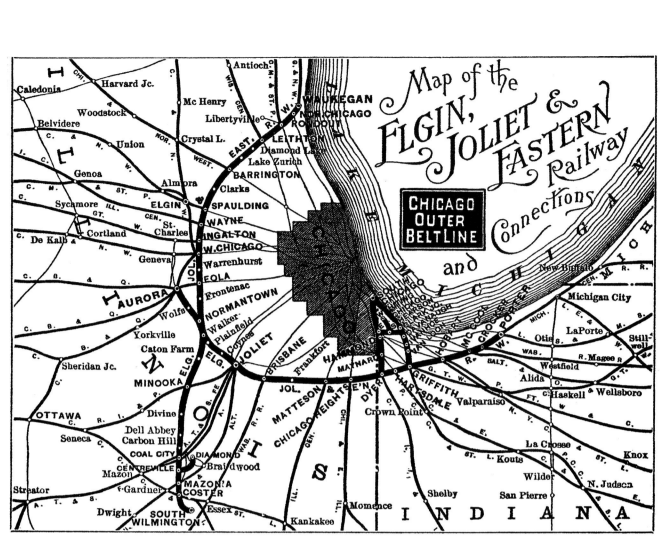

(Above) The EJ&E map from the 1906 *Official Guide of the Railways* shows the east end before Gary was completed. (Below) For years, the big Mikados of the EJ&E handled heavy transfers. No. 773 is shown about to get underway at West Chicago in June of 1936. Like a number of EJ&E engines, No. 773 later went to DM&IR. *(Harold K. Vollrath collection)*

Just as box cars went everywhere, so too the EJ&E's flat cars could be seen throughout the country. The first of EJ&E's modern, 50-ton steel flat cars were delivered in 1929 as EJ&E 8300–8374, notably with Andrews trucks. Within three years, they had been joined by 300 more cars of 50-foot length, and the series had become 6000–6374. Here is one of the cars from the first delivery, EJ&E 6041, photographed at Fort Bragg, North Carolina in October 1951, with military equipment being unloaded from the cars in the background.   *(Chet McCoid photo, Bob's Photo collection)*

After World War II, EJ&E purchased 200 more flat cars, 53 feet, 6 inches long, in the 6575–6774 series, built by American Car & Foundry in 1947. Shown here is repainted and relettered EJ&E 6657 on the Southern Pacific at Bayshore Yard, south of San Francisco, on July 28, 1964, with an interesting group of crates secured to its deck (all are stenciled "Caterpillar").   *(Chet McCoid photo, Bob's Photo collection)*

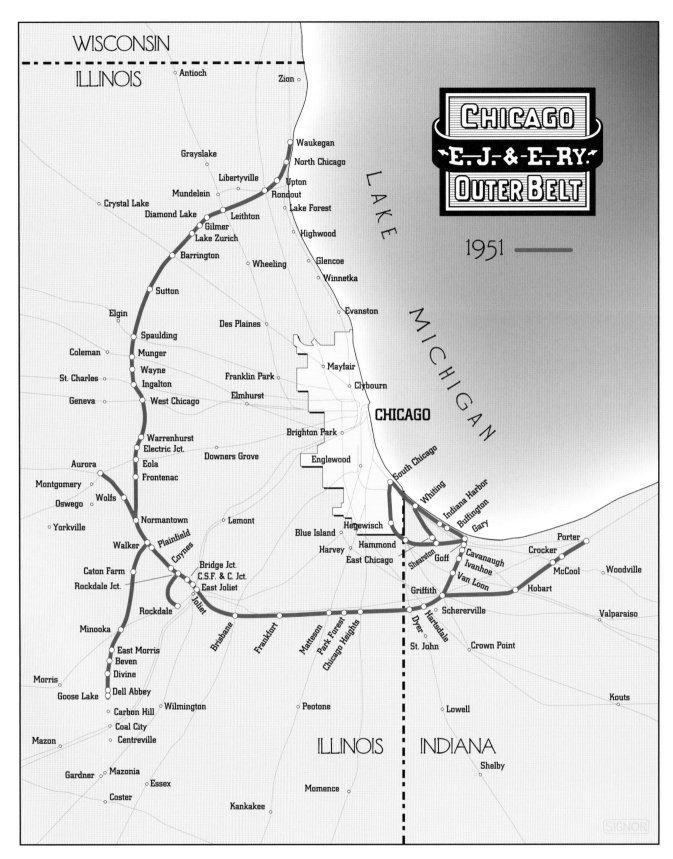

This map, depicting the lines of the EJ&E in 1951, approximately represents the maximum extent of the railroad.

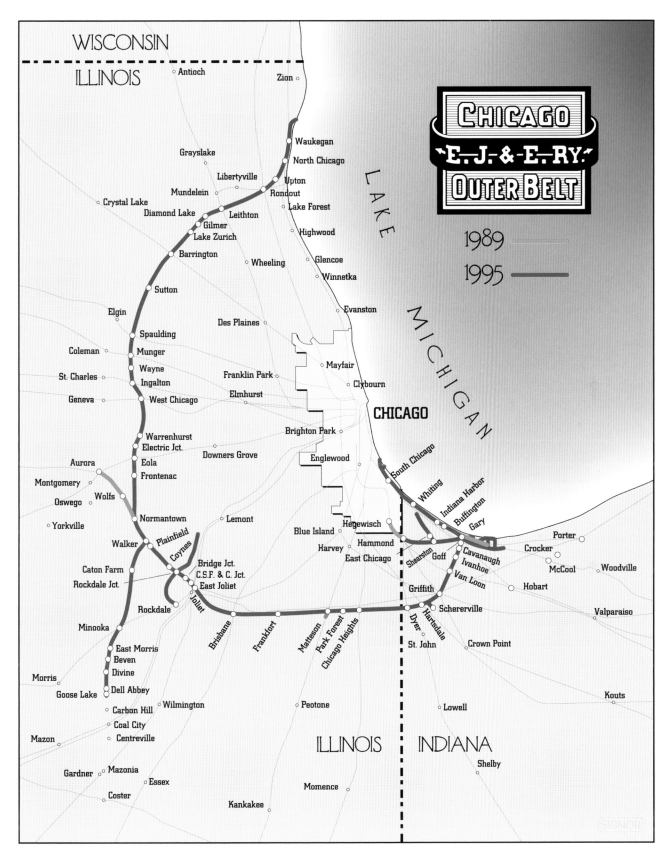

Parts of the EJ&E were abandoned in the late 20th century. This map summarizes these changes.

It is late 1945, and the EJ&E stills powers its freight trains with 2-8-2 Mikados, such as No. 749 shown here on the head end of a local freight at West Chicago, Illinois: the interchange point with the Chicago and North Western. In fact, note the C&NW wood-sheathed box car behind the tender. Practically every time freight and local made a stop at the C&NW interchange in the 1940s. As a side note, the 749 eventually went north to the Duluth, Missabe and Iron Range Railway (and was re-numbered 1315) for iron ore hauling.

(William S. Kuba)

Chapter 2

FREIGHT TRAINS FROM PORTER TO WAUKEGAN

THE EJ&E has been, and is, one extraordinary freight railroad! During the past 55 years since World War II, the railroad has served as many as 500 shippers at one time, and handled a wide variety of traffic from many manufacturers. Many of the industries that were served rated the title of "World's Largest," such as U.S. Steel's Gary Works. At one time, this plant was so busy that as many as 100 switch crews were assigned for intra-plant operations during a 24-hour period. (Much has changed since the 1950s.) Other such large facilities included Standard's oil refinery at Whiting (now British Petroleum) and Universal Atlas Cement Company's plant at Buffington, Indiana on the northwest side of Gary. The latter is no longer in operation. The EJ&E also served Inland Steel Company's Indiana Harbor plant at East Chicago, Indiana, and U.S. Steel's South Works plant at South Chicago.

Traditionally, the EJ&E has provided two basic services. One was (and is) the interchange services between eastern and western carriers around Chicago, while the other is the steel industry. Although the steel traffic has declined, partly because of the closure of U.S. Steel's South Works, the EJ&E is still a heavy freight hauler and continues to provide freight train services with a variety of operations and in the "J" tradition.

Over the past half century, the freight schedules were more or less designed to meet the needs of the steel companies, with the exception of those trains that operated almost exclusively for interchange traffic. The EJ&E literally connected with every railroad entering Chicago including terminal railroads within the city such as the Chicago Short Line, the Chicago, West Pullman and Southern, the Indiana Harbor Belt, and the Belt Railway of Chicago. In fact, people often confused the "Belt Railway" with the EJ&E's insignia advertising "Chicago Outer Belt."

Train Services and Operations

Prior to World War II, the EJ&E operated four trains in each direction between Joliet and Waukegan, plus a local as needed. This was an expanded schedule compared to situation at the worst of the Depression in 1933. In 1939, the eastbound train numbers (from Waukegan) were designated 4, 6, 10 and 2 in that order throughout the day. The westbound runs from Joliet to Waukegan included 3, 5, 9 and 11. Except for changing the number of train 2 to 12, this basic arrangement would literally remain in effect for over three decades. With the exception of placing the local, trains 17 and 18, on a daily-except-Sunday operation, the trains listed above provided excellent service for the American Steel and Wire Plant at Waukegan plus interchange service for all carriers crossing the 73-mile Western Subdivision between Waukegan and East Joliet Yard.

There were other freight train services on the Western Sub during the 1940s. Trains 7 and 8 operated as a turn from East Joliet. This pair of trains operated out of Joliet in the morning and ran to Spaulding and return. This was a Milwaukee Road connection, but made pick-ups and set-outs at other junctions as well. Another pair of trains operated between Joliet and Aurora as a turn, numbered 31 and 32.

Service on the Eastern Subdivision was more complicated. Three of the trains in each direction on the Western Sub actually originated or terminated at Porter, Indiana, a quiet community with extensive railroad action. Westbound trains 3, 5 and 9 ran the entire distance from Porter to Waukegan, while eastbounds 4, 6, and 10 did the honors to Porter. Each of these trains received extensive switching at East Joliet Yard. The scheduled stop ranged from 3 hours, 20 minutes to 7 hours, 25 minutes for the classification work. In reality, this sometimes took up to 12 hours, which was not uncommon during World War II. According to some very old records, individual cars often spent 48 hours moving from the Eastern to the Western Subdivision.

There were a number of other scheduled trains on the Eastern Subdivision. Eastbound the EJ&E operated trains 42 and 44 to Gary, and train 46 to Whiting. Westbound trains 43 and 49 provided the Gary to Joliet service, with train 41 coming from Whiting. The Gary trains handled finished steel products from Gary Works and South Works of U.S. Steel. Trains 41 and 46 served the oil industry in the Whiting area. Later these trains would run as an "extra," designated as the "Oiler."

During the early to mid-1950s, "The J" began revamping its scheduled freight train services to and from Porter. Trains 4 and 6, 9 and 11 provided the daily services with all interchanges, while trains 50 and 51 performed local services on a daily except Sunday basis. As mentioned previously, the "Oiler" became an extra in both directions and the number 49 was dropped on the Gary to Joliet run. It was replaced by the number 41.

The period from 1955 to 1965 saw only a few minor changes on the Western Subdivision. The Aurora trains operated as an extra turn out of Joliet and no longer carried the numbers 31 and 32. However, they were still listed in schedules provided for freight shippers. Former trains 7 and 8 between Joliet and Spaulding also became extra trains and operated when needed as a "Spaulding Turn." This meant that sometimes the train did not operate as far as Spaulding, but perhaps only as far as West Chicago or Eola. On the Eastern Subdivision, trains 4 and 6, and 9 and 11 continued to operated to and from Porter as well as their through operations on the Western Sub. The locals 50 and 51 were discontinued by 1965. On the other hand, trains 41 and 42 were reclassified as local freight trains between Joliet and Gary, and operated as Third Class trains. Trains 43 and 44 continued to provide through train services with the exception of picking up and setting out at various interchanges.

The closing of various mills at Waukegan, Joliet and even Duluth, Minnesota had a dramatic effect upon the traffic levels of the EJ&E. In the mid-1970s, the Western Subdivision had but one pair of daily freight trains, numbers 5 and 6, and one pair of daily except Sunday locals, trains 9 and 10. The Eastern Subdivision had one pair of scheduled trains, numbers 41 and 42, the daily

local freight between Gary and Joliet. Other assignments ran or operated as extras including the line to Porter, which saw but one train in each direction on a daily basis.

The Eastern Subdivision also played host to a group of trains that operated as turns or for unit trains movements of coal. These trains operated between Gary or Kirk Yard and such points as Hartsdale, Chicago Heights, Griffith and other locations. These coal train operations are covered in Chapter 3.

Service was also reduced to an "as-needed basis" for the Goose Lake Branch, Rockdale and what was left of the Aurora Branch, which since 1979 extended only as far as Wolfs. Later the last bit of mileage on the branch was taken up. (Refer to the various maps in Chapter 1.)

Train services on the former Gary Division to South Chicago and Whiting plus the "City Track" turn to Goff (through Gary) have been operated as "turns" out of Kirk Yard. One example during the 1970s through the 1980s included a local train to serve various industries in East Chicago and Whiting, with still another local train for Hammond, Hegewisch and 98th Street in South Chicago (not to be confused with the Lake Front line). Although these trains did not serve any steel mills directly, they did serve related industries including steel mill company supply and distribution warehouses.

The Lake Front line between Kirk Yard and South Chicago saw a substantial amount of traffic, and was double track with automatic block signals. The 12.37-mile section of the Gary Division was (is) entirely within Yard Limits, and the trains were operated without timetable schedules, clearance forms or train orders. The types of trains once included trains of hot metal from Gary Works to South Works, coke, inbound supplies and outbound steel products and sometimes even ore trains. There was also interchange traffic for the Chicago Short Line, the Indiana Harbor Belt and the Belt Railway of Chicago at various points on the Lake Front line.

The third route out of Kirk Yard was known as the "City Track," which extended through the City of Gary to a connection with the Chicago, South Shore and South Bend Railroad at Goff. This interchange was about two miles east of the South Shore station in downtown Gary. In between these two points, the J served a team track, a cement company and what was once known as the Pittsburgh Screw and Bolt Company. Train service on this line was always once a day, usually during the evening. In fact, to this writer's knowledge, the only time two trains operated on the line during a daily basis was during the construction of the Indiana Toll Road in the mid-1950s. (However, coal movements over the line for

EJ&E 2-8-2 No. 759 flies white flags handling an extra freight at Hammond, Indiana on the 98th Street Branch of the Eastern Subdivision of the Joliet Division. The 98th Street Branch covered the main line from Griffith, Indiana all the way to 98th Street in South Chicago. (The main line to Gary in 1945 extended from Cavanaugh (about nine miles from Griffith) to Kirk Yard in Gary, a distance of 3.6 miles and part of the Gary Division at that time.) *(Harold K. Vollrath collection)*

A Baldwin DT 6-6-1000/2, No. 113, handles a freight through Dyer, Indiana on September 6, 1950. The train has made a stop, as Dyer was an interchange point with the Monon Railroad. *(J. Michael Gruber collection)*

interchange with the South Shore have increased traffic frequency on the City Track. See Chapter 3)

Gary Works

One of the important components of the EJ&E freight services is the Gary Works intra-plant operation. The railroad has provided an effective switching service for U.S. Steel for decades. The railroad handles molten iron from the blast furnaces to the Basic Oxygen Furnaces (or BOF) for conversion into steel. This also involves the movement of coke from the coke plant on the far eastern side of the Gary Works facilities. Scrap steel is also brought into the BOF plant for part of the steelmaking process. Once the slab steel is produced, it must then be transported to other areas of the complex. Steel is moved to the Plate Mill for creating plate steel for building heavy equipment, including ships. "Plate" is normally steel in thicknesses above one-quarter inch. Flat steel which is thinner than plate is called "sheet" and is created for appliances and a wide variety of other products for household and industrial use. This type of steel must be of a very high quality. Sheet steel is also sent to another section, the Tin Mill, to apply tin plating for cans and a variety of products.

The outbound steel traffic moves in three types of equipment depending upon the quality and the need for weather protection. Covered coil-steel cars carry high quality sheet steel, while open gondolas equipped with troughs handle hot-band steel (sheet or plate). Box cars handle the tin-plated steel.

The EJ&E also serves two other steel plants. One is Ispat-Inland (the former Inland mill, owned by Rotterdam-based Ispat International) at Indiana Harbor on the Lake Front line, and the other steel plant is ISG (the former LTV Steel mill), subsequently also purchased by Ispat. In addition to the integrated mills, the EJ&E also serves the Indiana Harbor Coke Company, which produces coke for the various mills. The J is currently handling steel, scrap and coke for ISG Steel. Thus steel products continue to be a solid percentage of the EJ&E's traffic and marketing mix.

Moving into the 21st century, the EJ&E continues to provide a high quality freight service along its main line between Gary, Joliet and Waukegan. The railroad now operates two manifest trains in each direction between Joliet and Kirk Yard as well as "Turn" job between Kirk Yard and Matteson. The Kirk Yard-Matteson train is designated the KSW1, while the Gary-Joliet runs are referred to as the "Line Train" and the "Night Flyer."

Carload traffic is still an important part of the EJ&E's traffic mix. All carload traffic from interchanges and local industries goes to Kirk Yard for classification and blocking for the various railroad connections. The cars are blocked according to destination at the hump yard and assembled into outbound trains. The "Line Train" departs at 1:00 PM daily for Joliet, making all necessary stops for interchanging cars to their respective connections, with the "Night Flyer" departing Gary after midnight for a morning delivery in Joliet.

Ballast and stone traffic is another important ingredient of the traffic mix. The J operates a tri-weekly service to Material Service Corporation's quarry. Traffic includes seasonal loads for Peter Baker and Son's asphalt production plant at Rondout, Illinois as well as ballast for Metra and the EJ&E's own Maintenance of Way Department. Traffic levels can be as high as 50 cars on any given day in the spring and summer months.

Another very interesting facet of J freight services now involves haulage and trackage rights services. It is an interesting railroad operation involving through train services, including motive power from the participating railroads. This type of operation reduces transit time for freight moving through the Chicago area, as well as reducing area train congestion. (Yes, there is a traffic congestion problem on a number of rail routes through Chicago. New construction and rail line realignment is now taking place within Chicago. With the EJ&E's line around Chicago, and the new routing patterns, the traffic congestion problem will be solved and Chicago will continue to be North America's Railroad Center.)

Today the Canadian National (Grand Trunk Western and Illinois Central routes) operates trains between Griffith and Matteson. Still another CN operation involves trains between Leithton and Munger between the Wisconsin Division (former Wisconsin Central and the Illinois Central's former Chicago Central routes).

The Canadian National also has a daily westbound train from Griffith to Joliet destined for the Burlington Northern & Santa Fe. In addition, BNSF may operate trackage rights trains between Joliet (ATSF) and Eola (BN). Solid auto-rack trains also operate between West Chicago (UP/C&NW) and Griffith destined to the Canadian National's Grand Trunk Western line.

The new Haulage and Trackage Rights operations are bringing new levels of diversity with a wide variety of motive power and new levels of train traffic on the EJ&E. One could say that the EJ&E is the base line for new, faster, and more effective means for traffic interchange. It goes far beyond simply the efficiency level.

Except for the coal and ore trains, and some through trains from Gary to Joliet, many of the road trains make frequent stops for switching. As mentioned in Chapter 1, the EJ&E was once double track from Kirk Yard to East Joliet Yard. Because of the frequent stops, it was once considered to add a third track with Centralized Traffic Control for a substantial portion of the Eastern Subdivision. Eventually a steady decline in the health of the steel industry precluded such plans. The Eastern Subdivision is presently (2003) double track between Gary and Matteson, and single track beyond to Joliet and Waukegan. Automatic Block Signal systems are in operation for much of the route.

It can be said that the EJ&E train services, although less frequent on some route segments, are no less dramatic in the 2000s than they were over fifty years ago. Granted that steam and the Baldwin center cabs and covered wagon diesel units are gone, but the colorful SD38s and other modern power cover the entire territory from Gary to Joliet and Waukegan.

Timetable sheets illustrating the Freight Train Schedules for the years 1945, 1956, and 1976 are presented in Appendix 2. ❑

EJ&E No. 916 is westbound with an extra freight operating as a "Griffith Turn" out of Kirk Yard in Gary for interchanging delivery to the Chesapeake and Ohio at Griffith on this September day in 1963. The 916 is about to cross the Grand Trunk Western double track main line in the foreground. The C&O tracks are to the right of the photo. The switch for the Porter line is behind the Train Order signal to the right of the double track EJ&E main line. The "TO" sign is an indicator that it is a train order signal and not an interlocking signal governing the junction.

(William S. Kuba)

A westbound freight with a switch engine and a rebuilt (EMD) Baldwin Center Cab approach the Griffith station and yard. The westbound is from Gary and en route to Joliet. The train is No. 43, which was the morning time freight departure from Gary to Joliet. This photo was the basis for the frontispiece watercolor art.   *(Russ Porter)*

Two rebuilt Baldwin Center Cabs rebuilt by EMD are handling a freight at Joliet. There was a great deal of freight traffic in and out of Joliet during the 1960s, and there still is. During the mid-1960s, the EJ&E had four scheduled freight trains in each direction on the Eastern Subdivision of the Joliet Division (Two Gary-East Joliet, two Porter-East Joliet), and five scheduled trains in each direction between East Joliet and Waukegan on the Western Sub. This photo by Russ Porter was typical of some of the motive power consists heading up the trains on both subdivisions, east and west.   *(Russ Porter)*

Baldwin Center Cab No. 924 is picking up two cars from the former C&O off the interchange trackage at Griffith, Indiana.

(Russ Porter)

West Chicago was, and still is an important junction point for a wide variety of freight traffic between the J and the Chicago and North Western, now the Union Pacific main line to the West Coast. An eastbound "J" interchange freight from Waukegan is moving across the triple-track C&NW main line in this June, 1981 photo.

(Terry Hand)

A switch engine No. 303 and the center cab 903 is rolling by the Griffith Tower after setting out an interchange cut for the C&O yard. The two units are returning to their train and will continue running westbound after coupling up. *(William S. Kuba)*

EJ&E SW1200s numbers 304 and 301 have teamed up to bring an interchange of steel and other steel products for the Grand Trunk Western at Griffith. This "Griffith Turn" has a substantial number of GTW coiled steel cars in the consist on this September day in 1969. The train is crossing the GTW and Erie-Lackawanna/C&O diamonds just to the east of Griffith depot. The tower is to the right of the photo. *(William S. Kuba)*

The Elgin, Joliet and Eastern Railway

It is September, 1969, and William Kuba has caught the rebuilt Baldwin 909 passing the Griffith Yard Office. Although it is not 100 percent certain, this may be train 11 coming off the Porter line en route to East Joliet. Griffith was a favorite location for rail photography with three double track mainline crossings at grade: the EJ&E, GTW, and the joint E–L/C&O, plus the single-track line of the New York Central's subsidiary, the Joliet & Northern Indiana, which extended from East Gary, Indiana to Joliet. The J&NI was actually part of the Michigan Central. *(William S. Kuba)*

EJ&E No. 600, a long-end-forward SD9, is shown handling a local freight at Hammond, Indiana on a rather warm February 16, 1970. Note the orange and green color scheme applications on the long end and the placement of the bell.
(Owen Leander photo, J. Michael Gruber collection)

There is no snow on the ground, which is typical of Northern Indiana winters in this December, 1988 portrait of an eastbound EJ&E steel freight bound for Bethlehem Steel, which was located east of Gary, Indiana. The pair of DM&IR SD9s powering the freight are rolling over the Chicago, South Shore and South Bend Railroad just east of Gary, and next to the combined highways U.S. 12 and 20. Note the electric catenary wires overhead. *(Terry Hand)*

This photo of an EJ&E freight near Hartsdale (south of Hammond, Indiana) on the Eastern Subdivision illustrates part of the traffic patterns and flow over the J. Note the consist of coiled steel cars behind the SD38s 652 and 669. *(Terry Hand)*

In these two views, SD38-2s Numbers 665 and 661 are powering an eastbound local freight through Griffith in August, 1987. The train was en route from East Joliet to Kirk Yard in Gary. *(both photos, Patrick C. Dorin)*

A westbound freight running from Gary to East Joliet is rolling through Griffith with two cabooses on the rear end in August 1987. One of the cars is deadheading back to Joliet to balance the number of cars between terminals. *(Patrick C. Dorin)*

Although the caboose 509 is in the shadow, it is bringing up the rear of an EJ&E freight crossing the former Pennsylvania Railroad tracks at Hartsdale, Indiana on a superb Sunday afternoon in June, 1991. *(Terry Hand)*

THE ELGIN, JOLIET AND EASTERN RAILWAY

SD38 No. 652 is switching freight at the East Joliet Yard in this January, 1992 portrait toward the end of the daylight hours in a winter's day.

(Terry Hand)

SD38 No. 650 is switching freight cars for interchange at Chicago Heights on a pre-spring day in March, 1993. Chicago Heights was a multiple interchange point between the EJ&E and the Milwaukee Road, Louisville and Nashville, Chicago and Eastern Illinois, and the Chicago Heights Terminal and Transfer Railroad.

(Terry Hand)

Coal traffic has been a major part of the EJ&E traffic mix since its very beginning, and continues to be so in the 21st century. Most of the coal traffic is bound for either power plants or the coking plants at the steel mills in Gary. A pair of SD38-2s, the 668 and 657, head up a coal train headed for Gary Works in August, 1987. The eastbound train is crossing the former Nickel Plate Railroad (later Norfolk & Western) tracks at Van Loon on the Eastern Subdivision. The train consists of Norfolk & Western 100-ton capacity hopper cars loaded with metallurgical coal. This is a double-track section of the Eastern Sub.   *(both, Patrick C. Dorin)*

Chapter 3

COAL DRAGS AND UNIT TRAINS

THE EJ&E was not normally considered a "coal" railroad, but the Eastern Subdivision to and from Kirk Yard was—and is—truly a coal railroad of major proportions. Historically over the history of the J, the railroad also handled a substantial amount of coal traffic for local coal yards throughout the entire railroad. The small coal yards provided coal for home heating for many years extending into the 1960s. By that time, gas furnaces were replacing the cumbersome coal shoveling and other work connected with home heating. Coal was also handled for the electric utilities, which turned into a traffic pattern of substantial growth for the EJ&E and many other railroad lines. An even larger percentage of the coal traffic were the train loads of metallurgical coal for the steel industry at Gary, South Chicago and other steel making facilities within the Chicago–Gary Corridor along the Lake Front line.

The EJ&E was also a long-distance coal hauler. Because of the work of the Calumet and Blue Island in 1893 and its consolidation with the Chicago, Lake Shore and Eastern in 1897, which in turn became part of the EJ&E System, the J became heavily involved in metallurgical coal and limestone from central and southern Illinois. The trackage rights agreement permitted the EJ&E to handle empties only southbound, and the coal and limestone loads northbound over the Chicago and Eastern Illinois and the Chicago, Terra Haute and Southeastern. The CTH&SE was part of the Milwaukee Road system.

The trackage rights routing began at milepost 27.1 with a connecting line from the EJ&E to the C&EI near what was once Jay Tower at Chicago Heights. The routing moved south toward the Kankakee River Valley. After crossing the old Kankakee Belt Line and the river, the Coal Road route diverted from the main line at Momence Junction. The line continued off to the Southeast along the main line to Rossville Junction, which was the C&EI's milepost 107. The CLS&E had constructed a rail yard and engine facilities at Rossville Junction, which was 80 miles south of Jay Tower on the C&EI.

The coal train operations were quite interesting. There were 2 or 3 trains a day from Gary or Joliet. EJ&E crews would bring the empty trains to Rossville Junction yard. At Rossville Junction, the empty hopper cars were switched into local trains for both the Westville District in Illinois, and the Jackson area in Indiana.

The Westville District local runs made an interesting circle trip. The trains departed Rossville through Danville for a number of mines including the Vermilion, the Peabody, and the Bunseville in the Westville District. The EJ&E assigned a switch engine and crews at Westville to handle the mine run switching.

After the Westville District trains exchanged the empties for the coal loads, the trains continued west on the C&EI to Sidell Junction. At that point, the operations turned northward on the Sidell Branch for a limestone quarry at Casparis Spur, which was located about two miles north of Jamaica and near Fairmont, Illinois. The EJ&E did assign a switch crew for the Casparis Spur limestone operations. Upon picking up the limestone loads, the combination coal and limestone trains would roll northward back to Rossville Junction completing a 73 mile circle operation.

The Jackson trains operated southbound on the C&EI through Alvin Junction and Bismarck to a junction known as BX Tower. At this point, the Jackson trains turned on to the C&EI's Starr Cutoff, which connected with the CTH&SE bypassing Danville. The EJ&E regained the

Power company coal traffic can be observed on virtually all segments of the J. This locomotive, SD9 No. 611, is working as a rear helper engine on a power company unit coal train heading for a plant near Gary, Indiana. The train is departing Griffith, Indiana on the Eastern Subdivision in August, 1987. Note the type of 100-ton coal hoppers ahead of No. 611.   (Patrick C. Dorin)

Coal train traffic arrives in both power company equipment and railroad-owned equipment. Note the post-Conrail New York Central reporting marks on these 100-ton CSX coal hoppers, which were part of a coal train interchanged with the EJ&E.

(Frank Schnick)

An ex-DM&IR diesel engine, now lettered for The J in the DM&IR color scheme, is pulling a train of empty coal hoppers from Gary Works into Kirk Yard. The train was unloaded at the coke plant, and the empties will now return to the mines for more metallurgical coal on this day in October 2003. *(Patrick C. Dorin)*

A string of Norfolk and Western coal hoppers are being moved over the hump at Kirk Yard in Gary during October, 2003. The N&W cars carry the NW reporting marks and the Norfolk Southern insignia. *(Patrick C. Dorin)*

The Will County power plant of Midwest Generation (just north of Joliet) receives coal in unit trains, with the EJ&E providing delivery of the loads, and picking up the empties. This photo from October 2003 shows the Will County power plant coal train yard north of Joliet. Note the EJ&E caboose at left. *(Patrick C. Dorin)*

C&EI main line at Walz east of Danville. From that point, the trains continued for another 36 miles to the Jackson area. C&EI crews did the mine switching on the various spurs and mines and assembled the loads for the EJ&E's northbound operations. The Jackson District operations were discontinued in 1932 due to the Depression. All of the coal and limestone operations over the C&EI were discontinued in 1948.

Moving through the later part of the 20th century into the 1980s and '90s, the company's coal traffic expanded with new movements of unit trains of coal from the BN (now BNSF) and the C&NW (now UP), whereas most of the coal once originated in Illinois, Indiana and throughout the east.

Although some metallurgical coal for northwest Indiana arrives via Spaulding and Eola, from the Canadian Pacific and the BNSF respectively, most of this coal traffic arrives via Curtis from the CSX and Van Loon from the Norfolk Southern. Both points are located in Gary. Such coal traffic is also received from the Canadian Pacific Railway at Spaulding. This connection is the former Milwaukee Road as well as the Soo Line Railroad.

Unit trains of energy coal are destined for a variety of power plants throughout the South Chicago — Gary and Joliet areas. Power plants include the Northern Indiana Public Service Company plant near Gary, State Line Energy at Hammond, Midwest Generation's Will County plant at Romeoville. Other traffic is handled via haulage or trackage rights to Midwest Generation's plant north of Joliet or Waukegan for the Union Pacific.

Historically, the EJ&E interchanged coal with the old C&O at Griffith, which was eventually replaced by a B&O movement—and later as CSX; the former New York Central at Hartsdale, which eventually became a Conrail connection, the former Monon at Dyer, Indiana, both the former Milwaukee Road and Chicago and Eastern Illinois railroads at Chicago Heights, and finally to a limited extent, the former Wabash at Brisbane.

The EJ&E once handled substantial amounts of coal from what was known as the Coal City Branch. Virtually all of this coal, except for steam motive power fuel, flowed eastward to Kirk Yard for delivery to the coke plant operations at U.S. Steel at the east side of Gary.

The operations have always been relatively simple. The connecting railroad delivers the coal to the designated tracks at the various connections. The EJ&E then operated a train of empties to the connection, picked up the loads and returned to Kirk Yard. At Kirk Yard, the trains are either constructively placed or forwarded to a small yard called "The River Yard" ahead of the U.S.

Steel Coke Plant's rotary dumper according to the needs of the plant. Various cuts of cars are made up into transfers that depart the River Yard and operate over the Dixie Lead through the north end of Gary. The Dixie Lead parallels the former New York Central and Baltimore and Ohio main lines, and skirts the south side of the steel mills. Since this same line provides the lead for the Kirk Yard hump, train movements were and are extensive.

Upon delivery to the coke plant, the cars are run through a dumper and made up for return to Kirk Yard. Meanwhile, the coke ovens heat the coal in the absence of oxygen, driving off volatiles and tar and converting it to coke for use in steelmaking. The coke is loaded into special coke hopper cars, known as coke racks, and handled to the blast furnaces. This is an intra-plant movement to the steelmaking blast furnaces. The EJ&E at one time also handled coke via Kirk Yard for movement up the Lake Front line to South Chicago.

Back to the empty coal car movements. When the cars are ready to be returned to Kirk Yard, the cars are picked up. The train is then inspected and prepared for the trip back to the interchange connection, and the cycle repeats itself. This is one of the least complex operations on the EJ&E, and makes up truly the only non-stop train operations on the railroad.

Besides the inbound metallurgical coal for the U.S. Steel coke plant, the EJ&E also participates in operating unit coke trains with several railroads. The trains arrive at Kirk Yard and are then moved to either U.S. Steel, Ispat-Inland or Ispat-ISG where they are emptied and returned promptly to the connecting participating run-through railroad.

There have been some variations in the movement of coal and coke on the EJ&E. For example, during the 1960s and '70s, U.S. Steel shipped coke from the Duluth, Minnesota Works to Gary and South Chicago. This movement was interchanged from either the Soo Line, Chicago & North Western or the Milwaukee Road for transportation to the ultimate destination. Another movement of coke came in the form of solid trains from the Clairton Works in Pennsylvania. These trains operated via a Pittsburgh & Lake Erie / New York Central (Penn Central / Conrail) or a Nickel Plate Road (Norfolk & Western / Norfolk Southern) routings and a connection with the EJ&E at Pine and Van Loon respectively. These long unit trains of Bessemer and Lake Erie Railroad hopper cars made a colorful sight on the EJ&E.

Since the 1970s through to the present time (2004), 100 percent of the coal traffic on the EJ&E is for the steel industry and electric power plants. There is a substantial amount of coal traffic as the railroads moved forward through the late 20th century, there were several changes.

The electric power plant coal traffic is phenomenal. At the present time (2004), there is average of 15 unit trains per month from the Union Pacific at West Chicago (former C&NW), and from the UP at Chicago Heights (former Chicago & Eastern Illinois and the Missouri Pacific) for delivery to the Northern Indiana Public Service Company, known as NIPSCO. The coal originates from the Powder River Basin as well as the Illinois coal fields. The trains are handled with run-through power from the Union Pacific. It is not unusual to see UP and Southern Pacific power at Kirk Yard in Gary. Once the unit trains have arrived at Kirk Yard, the trains are then handled over the City Track routed through the north end of Gary to a connection with the Chicago South Shore at Goff, which in turn delivers for NIPSCO.

Unit coal trains also run through to Waukegan from the UP at West Chicago, while still another coal train service involves West Chicago for delivery to the Wisconsin Central (former Soo Line, now part of the Canadian National) at Leithton for delivery to a power plant in the Green Bay, Wisconsin area.

Coal trains destined for Midwest Generation in Will County, just north of Joliet, come from the Union Pacific at West Chicago and the Burlington Northern Santa Fe at Eola (the former BN). There can be as much as one coal train a day for this plant. There are also 20 to 30 coal trains per month for the Midwest Generation plant at The Plaines Station.

Coal trains on the EJ&E were not solid trains of "J" hopper cars, but rather equipment from the C&O, L&N (Seaboard and later CSX) and many other carriers. (Although the EJ&E once owned and operated a fleet of 50-, 70- or 75-ton capacity coal hoppers, the equipment was used primarily for limestone, coke and various local miscellaneous traffic.) Now all of the coal traffic is handled in equipment from the CSX, BNSF, and UP. It is interesting to note that much of the coal equipment from CSX now carries the NYC reporting marks formerly used by New York Central. Still other equipment includes private cars carrying the reporting marks of the various utilities, such as CWEX (originally Commonwealth Edison marks, used for Midwest Generation), NORX (NIPSCO), etc.

All of the coal business is interline received. There is some bridge traffic with unit trains of coal occasionally handled from western carriers to eastern lines. The company has not served any coal mines since the line to Coal City, Illinois was abandoned. Still, the EJ&E can be considered a major coal carrier, with an average annual coal tonnage of over 16.5 million tons, not including overhead trackage rights movements.

The photographs in this chapter illustrate the types of coal train traffic on the EJ&E, which in turn adds another level of diversity of traffic levels for the railroad. It is indeed a primary coal hauler. ❏

At right, EJ&E center cab No. 924 arrives at Griffith, Indiana with a "Griffith Turn" consisting of empty C&O coal hoppers for the C&O, and this westbound has stopped for the home signal for the crossings as Erie-Lackawanna's time freight 2nd No. 74 races across the EJ&E tracks. As a side note: E-L's 2nd No. 74 is powered by two Delaware, Lackawanna & Western RS-3s with a freshly repainted Erie-Lackawanna PA-1 running between the two RS-3s.   *(William S. Kuba)*

This train is on the Wisconsin Central, approaching its connection with the EJ&E. The photo illustrates the DM&IR ore cars that frequently operated over the J. The loads are natural ore, which by the 1995 date of this photo was becoming quite rare. However, remarkably, it can still happen from many of the stockpiles on the Mesabi Range. *(David C. Schauer)*

There are many stories to tell about the all-rail ore movements. The originating railroad motive power often operated through to the final destination on the EJ&E. In this case, Union Pacific motive power will be operating all the way to Kirk Yard in Gary with its all-rail ore train from U.S. Steel's Minntac taconite pellet plant on the Mesabi. There are 105 loads on this train with the UP power on the DM&IR's Mesabi Division main line near Proctor, Minnesota. Winter is still in full swing on this February day in 2004 and the all-rail ore trains are moving full speed ahead. *(David C. Schauer)*

Chapter 4

ORE TRAINS FROM THE LAKE SUPERIOR REGION

THE EJ&E has played a major role with the all-rail ore train operations from the Lake Superior Region since the late 1940s. The history of EJ&E ore hauling actually began during the early 1920s when the company handled approximately 1 million tons per year for a mill in Joliet. This operation was long gone by the 1940s.

The company has provided two types of service, interline received for Gary Works and other mills, and bridge traffic. Most of the ore for Gary Works comes from mines on the Duluth, Missabe & Iron Range Railway in Northern Minnesota. For much of the time during the 1960s through the 1980s, the traffic moved via either the Soo Line, the Milwaukee Road or the Chicago & North Western from the Duluth or Superior interchanges to connections with the "J" at Roundout, Leithton, Upton or Barrington. The company handled the train loads directly to the mills—either South Chicago or Gary Works—through Kirk Yard. When the cars were emptied, the train was returned to interchange carrier at one of the above points.

Bridge traffic ore was and is handled by the EJ&E from the western carriers, such as the Burlington Northern (now BNSF) and the eastern carriers, such as the former Nickel Plate, Baltimore & Ohio, New York Central, Erie-Lackawanna, and the Chesapeake & Ohio. As this is being written in 2004, there are but two eastern carriers, the Norfolk Southern and CSX.

The new regional railroad, the Wisconsin Central, took over part of the former Soo Line routes in Wisconsin in 1987. Since the early 1990s, the WC is handling much of the all-rail ore for U.S. Steel and interchanges the ore trains with the EJ&E at Leithton. The Wisconsin Central is now part of the Canadian National Railways.

The Canadian National has not only purchased the Wisconsin Central, but as of May, 2004, has also added the DM&IR to its system. This CN all-rail ore train is en route to Gary, Indiana with 93 cars on March 23, 2004. The train will still have its motive power upon its arrival at Kirk Yard in Gary.

(David C. Schauer)

The Chicago & North Western (now the Union Pacific) has also handled all-rail ore for interchange with the EJ&E for either Gary Works or other eastern destinations. The Barrington interchange is no longer used for ore interchange because part of the line through Wisconsin has been abandoned.

The Soo Line, now part of the Canadian Pacific, has played a very minor role in ore traffic. The Soo Line operates the former Milwaukee Road trackage with the Roundout interchange.

When the Milwaukee Road handled all-rail ore movements during the 1960s, '70s and '80s, the trains consisted either of Milwaukee Road coal hopper cars or DM&IR ore cars. In a few cases, Milwaukee Road ore cars were handled in interchange ore trains from the Upper Peninsula of Michigan.

Prior to the mega-mergers, the EJ&E handled substantial amounts of ore from the western carriers to the eastern railroads, including the former Baltimore & Ohio and Chesapeake & Ohio (both now CSX), Nickel Plate Road, later Norfolk & Western (now part of the Norfolk Southern), Pittsburgh & Lake Erie / New York Central (Penn Central and then Conrail). The different railroads participated with a variety of coal hoppers from the eastern lines. This also included borrowed equipment from the C&EI, Missouri Pacific, and the Louisville & Nashville. These ore operations once operated with a very interesting variety of equipment.

As a side note, Gary Works sometimes received ore from other areas in Minnesota, such as Cuyuna Range during the 1950s. In this case, Soo Line ore cars instead of DM&IR cars would be seen at Gary, an unusual sight to say the least, but it did happen.

Moving into the 21st century, the all-rail ore trains on the EJ&E are made up of either DM&IR ore cars or the 100-ton coal hopper cars operated in ore service. Motive power can consist of EJ&E units on the J, or mixtures from the Wisconsin Central, Grand Trunk Western, Canadian National, Norfolk Southern, Union Pacific and CSX. On rare occasions even DM&IR power has run through to the J. Ore traffic now operates on a year-round basis instead of only during the winter season. As this is being written in April, 2004, there is some all-rail ore traffic operating from the DM&IR via the CN's Wisconsin Division (Wisconsin Central) and the Union Pacific. Thus ore traffic, although sometimes sporadic, can be quite interesting because of the diverse equipment and motive power for the various trains. ❏

Chapter 5

EAST JOLIET AND KIRK YARD

THE two strategic terminals for the EJ&E are the East Joliet Yard and Kirk Yard, located just to the west of the Gary Works complex. Both yards play a crucial role in the movement of freight between railroads and to and from U.S. Steel's Gary Works.

Although most freight classification is done at Kirk Yard, the EJ&E's Joliet Yard is still very active and is used to stage cars for Illinois River line industries as well as processing local Joliet industry movements. Cars are blocked according to the set-outs that need to be made as the trains depart from Joliet to Waukegan or intermediate points. Trains and equipment are also inspected at East Joliet.

East Joliet is also the home for the company repair shops for freight equipment. The shops are extensive and repair several pieces of equipment every month. Although major locomotive work is done in Gary at the Kirk Yard roundhouse, light running motive power repairs and monthly inspections are performed at Joliet.

The East Joliet facility also includes the general office building for the headquarters of the EJ&E. The building is known as the O&O building. The yellow brick building houses virtually all of the operating department, engineering, accounting and the numerous other departments and sub-departments required for effective operation of the railroad.

An EJ&E SD9M, No. 804 and a SD18 No. 616 are operating as multiple units (MU) and working the hump at Kirk Yard on this warm and delightful autumn day in October, 2003. As one can see, the units are former DM&IR units re-lettered for the EJ&E. The units were in the process of shoving a group of carloads of coiled steel over the hump for classification to different interchange connections along both the Eastern and Western Subdivisions. *(Patrick C. Dorin)*

Kirk Yard, on the other hand, is located at what is now the eastern point of the EJ&E. As mentioned above, the yard is adjacent to Gary Works and plays multiple roles for serving railroad shippers. Trains arriving at Kirk Yard include general freight trains with various types of freight for not only U.S. Steel, but other surrounding industries, and also the unit coal and coke trains.

The general freight must be switched for delivery to the appropriate receivers. Various types of switching assignments take cars to U.S. Steel and other companies.

Other assignments travel to South Chicago making deliveries en route to Inland Steel and other plants. Still others travel to Whiting to make deliveries to the former Standard (now BP) oil refinery and a variety of smaller industries. Returning, the assignments bring back new loads as well as empty cars. Upon arrival at Kirk Yard, the cars are switched according to destination interchange. The automatic hump yard configuration at Kirk allows a very effective and efficient handling of freight traffic for the EJ&E and its shippers. ❏

Switch engines, either alone or operated in multiple units, or with a slug, are assigned to Kirk Yard for switching, working the hump, or transfer service between the Yard and Gary Works. Assignments to other steel product plants, such as the Sheet and Tin Mill, also work with switch engines, the wide variety of EJ&E road-switchers, or both. Engine 459, shown here, is between switching assignments in this morning view at Kirk Yard. *(Patrick C. Dorin)*

The retarder at the down side of the hump leading into the classification part of Kirk Yard. *(Patrick C. Dorin)*

THE ELGIN, JOLIET AND EASTERN RAILWAY

The diesel power locomotive service facility at Kirk Yard. *(Patrick C. Dorin)*

Motive power laying over at Kirk Yard between main line freight operations as well as transfer duties for the City Track, South Chicago and other industrial switching assignments. *(Patrick C. Dorin)*

The RIP Track at Kirk Yard works throughout the day to handle a variety of small repairs as well as changing out wheels. Cars marked "Bad Order" are switched as quickly as possible to the RIP (Repair In Place) Track, especially loads, in order to minimize delays for shippers and receivers.

(Patrick C. Dorin)

Two SW1200s, the 305 and 306 are MU'd and performing a variety of switching duties at Kirk Yard on the October, 2003 day. The units are in the new green color scheme with the "J" insignia. Several people at Kirk Yard told the writer that they really enjoy the new colors.

(Patrick C. Dorin)

The East Joliet Yard is a crucial part of the J's distribution system for freight traveling over the Western and Eastern Subdivisions. Joliet is the division point between the two line segments. This view shows a freight arriving with two Baldwin center cabs for power. Note the railroad shops to the right of the photo.

(Russ Porter)

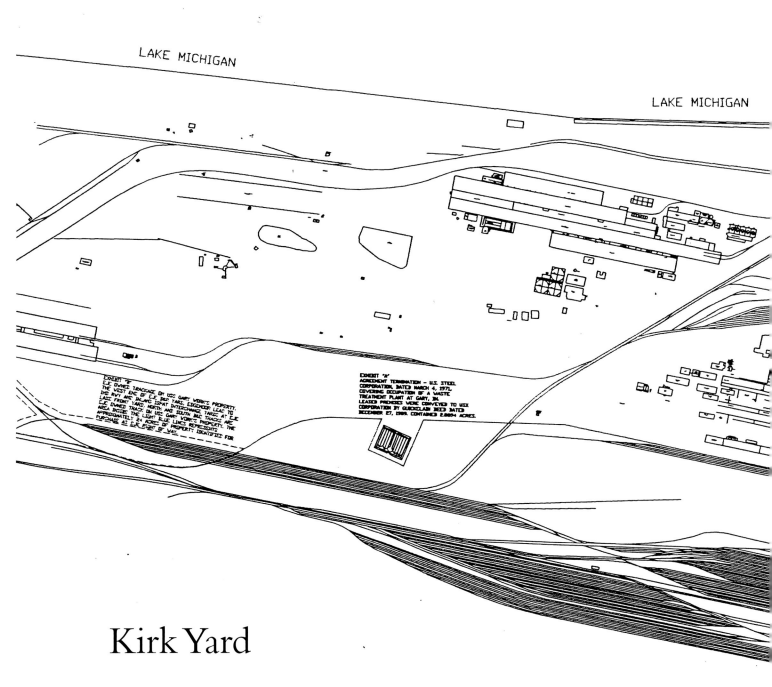

LAKE MICHIGAN

LAKE MICHIGAN

Kirk Yard

The numerous large structures between·
the yard tracks and Lake Michigan are of
U.S. Steel's Gary Works. Arrangement and
configuration of the mill buildings changed
from time to time. *(EJ&E map)*

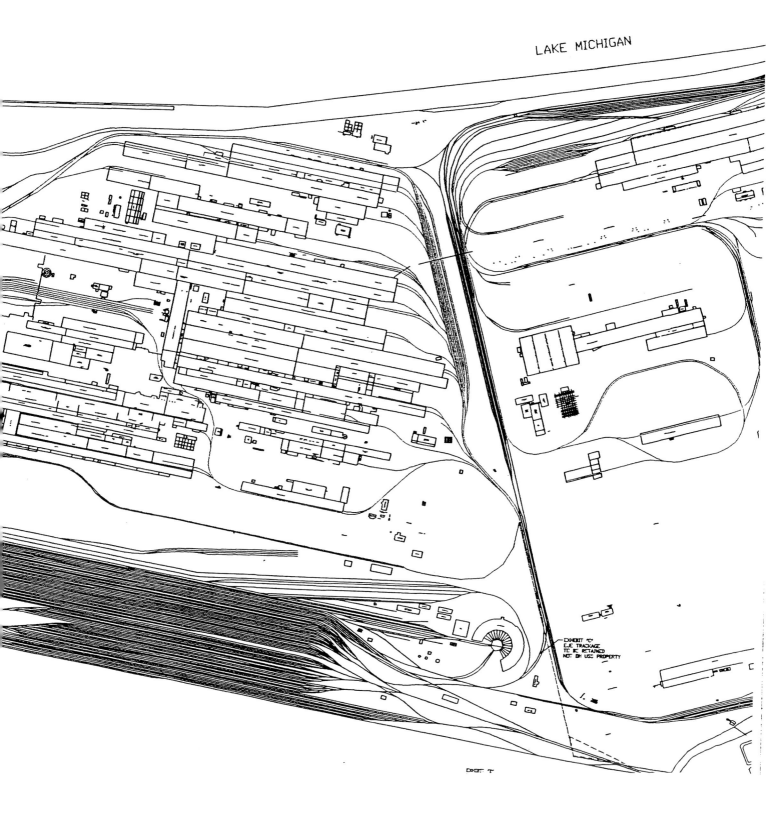

LAKE MICHIGAN

EXHIBIT "C"
EJE TRACKAGE
TO BE RETAINED
NOT BY USS PROPERTY

EXHIBIT "T"

SW1200 No. 322 is working the East Joliet Yard and is handling a caboose for a special switching move in these two October, 2003 portraits. *(Patrick C. Dorin)*

THE ELGIN, JOLIET AND EASTERN RAILWAY

Another switch engine is working the north end of the yard preparing a train for departure over the Western Subdivision. Note the overpass to the right of the photo which crosses the East Joliet Yard. *(Patrick C. Dorin)*

The East Joliet roundhouse continues to serve the diesel motive power as it did during the days of steam. Also, various minor types of repairs are handled at the facility. *(Patrick C. Dorin)*

Another October, 2003 view of the roundhouse shows a number of units between assignments at the facility. Two Belt Railway of Chicago switch engines were also at the facility for some repairs.

(Patrick C. Dorin)

The East Joliet motive power fueling and sanding facilities are near the roundhouse. Note the Union Pacific power to the right of the EJ&E locomotives on this October, 2003 day. UP power runs through on the EJ&E with unit coal trains.

(Patrick C. Dorin)

The EJ&E shops are also located at East Joliet. The shops provide maintenance and repairs for the wide variety of J equipment.

(Patrick C. Dorin)

One never knows what one might see at a railroad facility. It goes far beyond the rule to expect a train on any track at any time in either direction. In this case, former Metra Gallery Coaches are being stored at a facility adjoining the East Joliet Yard. The cars have been replaced by newer equipment on many of the Metra commuter passenger trains.

(Patrick C. Dorin)

Although all motive power operated at the two major EJ&E yards is now from Electro-Motive Division, there was a time when a number of Baldwin switchers were part of the motive power team. In this case, a Baldwin VO 1000, rebuilt by EMD, leads caboose No. 534 through the south end of the East Joliet yard on September 21, 1969.

(William S. Kuba)

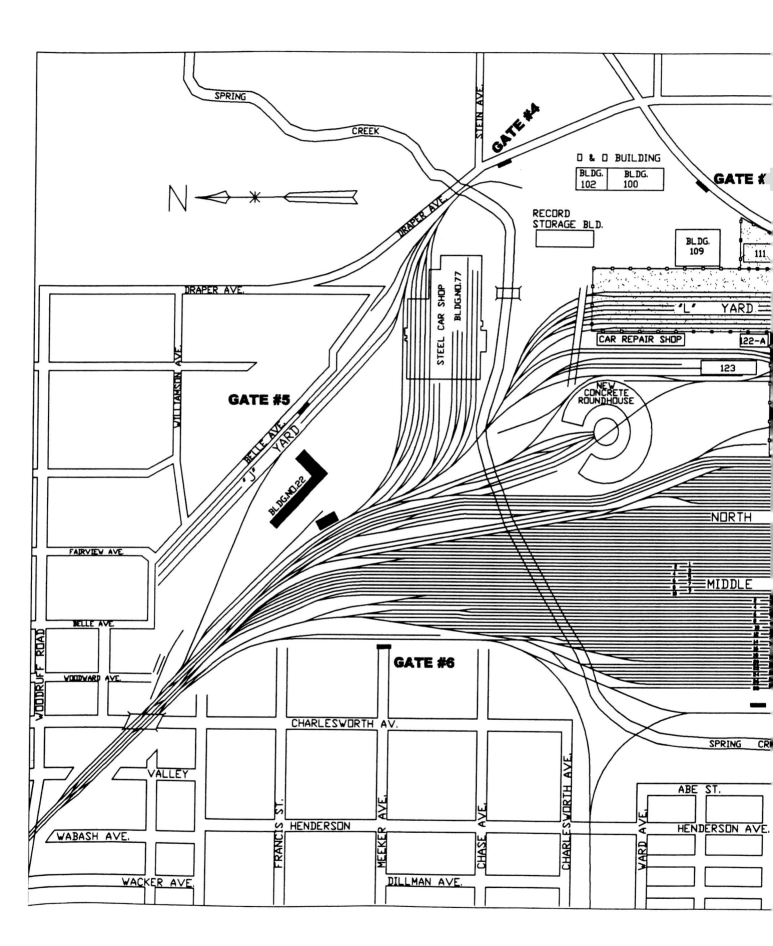

SPRING

CREEK

N

GATE #4

GATE #

STEIN AVE.

DRAPER AVE.

O & O BUILDING

BLDG.
102

BLDG.
100

RECORD
STORAGE BLD.

BLDG.
109

111

DRAPER AVE.

STEEL CAR SHOP   BLDG.NO.77

"L"   YARD

CAR REPAIR SHOP

122-A

123

WILLIAMSON AVE.

GATE #5

BELLE AVE.

"J"   YARD

NEW
CONCRETE
ROUNDHOUSE

BLDG.NO.22

NORTH

FAIRVIEW AVE.

MIDDLE

BELLE AVE.

WOODRUFF ROAD

WOODWARD AVE.

GATE #6

CHARLESWORTH AV.

SPRING CR

VALLEY

ABE ST.

WABASH AVE.

FRANCIS ST.

HENDERSON

MEEKER AVE.

CHASE AVE.

CHARLESWORTH AVE.

WARD AVE.

HENDERSON AVE.

WACKER AVE.

DILLMAN AVE.

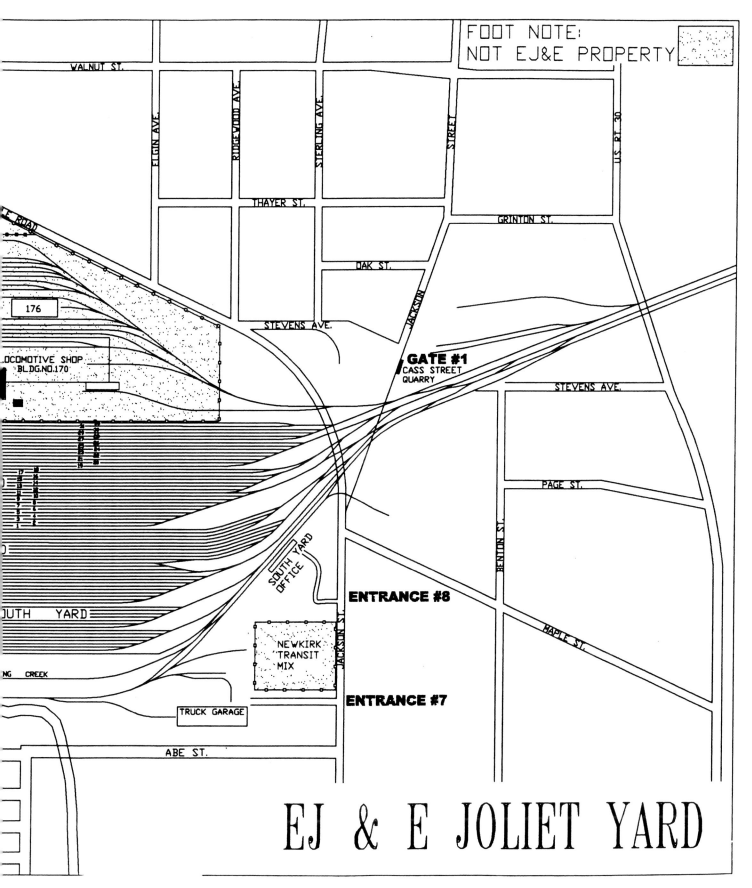

The East Joliet yard performed classification work for transfer and interchange cuts both eastward and westward. *(EJ&E map)*

It is 1936 and this business car train is powered by 2-8-0 No. 578. The train consists of the two business cars, numbers 50 and 40, that the EJ&E had owned and operated for several years. The white flags on No. 578 indicate that the train is operating as a passenger extra.

(EJ&E photo, Patrick C. Dorin collection)

The EJ&E dieselized much earlier than most other railroads, and subsequently, Alco road switchers were often used to power the business car specials. This May 1956 photo shows that there have been some interesting changes and additions to the business car fleet. No. 802 is heading up a four-car train instead of the two which were typical through the 1930s and '40s. The EJ&E acquired a heater car with a steam generator to provide steam for the passenger equipment. The second car is No. 40, while the third is a former Milwaukee Road dining car, now painted in Pullman green with Elgin, Joliet and Eastern lettering. The dining car was numbered 103. The final car is business car No. 50.

(EJ&E photo, Patrick C. Dorin collection)

Chapter 6

PASSENGER SERVICE ON THE EJ&E

NO one would ever think of the EJ&E as a passenger carrier, but indeed it once was. At one time the J provided a twice-daily passenger service between Joliet and Aurora, and for a brief period of time between Joliet and Waukegan, and Joliet and Porter. All passenger services were discontinued by 1907.

The company for many years maintained passenger tariffs between Porter and Waukegan and all stations in between. The local freight trains were permitted to carry revenue passengers in the caboose. On the Western Subdivision this meant trains 17 and 18 between Joliet and Waukegan with scheduled running times of 5 hours, 10 minutes westbound, and 4 hours, 45 minutes eastbound for the 73 mile run. On the Eastern Subdivision, trains 50 and 51 did the honors between Joliet and Porter, with schedules of 5 hours, 40 minutes eastbound, and 5 hours, 30 minutes westbound according to the July 8, 1956 schedules. The practice of carrying revenue passengers was discontinued around 1964. However, that did not mean the end of carrying passengers.

The company did from time to time operate a passenger extra as a Director's Special. The company owned during the early 1960s, one steam generator (heater) car, one dining car (formerly a 1937 streamlined Milwaukee Road dining car) and two business cars. One of the business cars was sold for a summer home, while the other remained in service for a period of time. The company continued to own and operate the steam generator car and dining car into the 1990s. The equipment was painted Pullman green with gold lettering.

Prior to the 1960s, the EJ&E operated a picnic special every summer from Gary to Joliet for company employees. The railroad would borrow passenger equipment for these annual runs. It was believed by the public in Gary that these trains were operated for fulfilling a legal requirement that the company must operate one passenger train per year over a portion of the railroad in order to remain an all-freight line. There were some stipulations in the original charter of the railway, which is why passengers were permitted to ride the caboose of the local trains.

The EJ&E operated regular passenger service only for a short time, as it was built primarily as a freight line to serve the heavy industry of the Chicago area as well as to serve as an important bridge carrier between railroads of the east and west.

Before closing, it may be mentioned that the January-February, 1979 issue of the magazine *J-Milepost* reported some rather interesting special passenger service for a

Elgin, Joliet and Eastern Railway Business Car No. 40

The car was constructed by the Pullman Company in 1902. The 72-foot, 4-inch car was of wood construction with arched wood sash for the windows, and double observation platforms. The interior of the car was decorated with Peruvian mahogany and oak. No. 40 was rebuilt in 1951. The arched windows were squared and the observation platform on the dining room end was removed. The dining room was expanded by 14 feet, making space for an additional four chairs. The car was modified again in the early 1980s when one of the staterooms was removed providing more space for the observation room. The car was eventually sold to the Russ Porter family. See drawings, this chapter, from *Railroad Model Craftsman*.

fair in Libertyville in September, 1901. The company operated regularly scheduled trains between Barrington and Libertyville, and Waukegan and Libertyville, September 4th through 6th. (See article reproduced on page 72.) In a strange way, one could say it was almost a prelude to the possibility of commuter rail service on the EJ&E— which could happen literally a century later!

METROPOLITAN RAIL:
A New Era of Passenger Service

Who would ever have thought that someday there might be regular passenger train service on the EJ&E back in the 1950s? Or the early 1990s for that matter! However, as highway and expressway congestion becomes more intense, making commuting complicated by increasing delays and stress problems, and pollution increases as a result of intense automobile travel and unexpected gridlock patterns, the EJ&E rail route has been considered and has been under study for potential "Around Chicago" routings. What does this mean?

Many commuters are now traveling from suburb to suburb for their employment. Possible end points for this new concept of commuter rail travel has included various short distances, such as Barrington to West Chicago and Aurora; and even the entire distance of the EJ&E from Waukegan to Gary, Indiana. In a way, it brings back a memory regarding passenger services on the EJ&E before 1907. (Especially since it is only railroad technology that can alleviate air and highway traffic congestion.)

Planning for the potential route includes new stations, parking lots, additional coordination with bus services, and some possible route modifications. For example, commuter trains off the EJ&E might transfer to the South Shore on the far west side of Gary. From there the trains would operate to a downtown station. Another possibility could include using the EJ&E trackage and bypassing Kirk Yard and running to downtown Gary. The EJ&E has a route that crosses Broadway on an overpass and is approximately one block from the South Shore passenger station for the Northern Indiana Commuter Transportation District.

Final decisions have not yet been made as of this writing in November, 2003; but do not be surprised if the EJ&E becomes part of the Metra commuter rail system in the near future. Push-pull commuter streamliners may well be launching a new era of passenger service on the Elgin, Joliet and Eastern Railway. ❏

In addition to the two business cars, the EJ&E also owned and operated an Instruction Car (*Mr. Safe J*) with an observation platform, giving it the look of a business car. The car was operated for various classes and instructional sessions on air brakes, motive power operations, safety programs and many other topics. Instruction Car No. 60, the former Plan 3959A sleeper-lounge car *Golden Beach*, was purchased from the Pullman Company in February 1955. *(Russ Porter photo, Patrick C. Dorin collection)*

Business car No. 50 is shown here coupled to dining car No. 103. This view shows the left side of the business car.

(Patrick C. Dorin collection)

This company photo was taken in May, 1959 on the far east side of the Gary Works steel mill complex of U.S. Steel. Locomotive 807 is powering the four-car train with dining car No. 103 behind the heater car, followed by business cars 50 and 40.

(EJ&E Photo, Patrick C. Dorin collection)

Business car No. 40 was originally constructed as a wooden car.

(EJ&E photo, Patrick C. Dorin collection)

Interior view of the lounge-observation area of business car No. 50. The two views illustrate the type of seating arrangement as well as the location of the door to the right side of the photo at one end of the lounge, while the other view looks toward the center of the car.

(Russ Porter photos, Patrick C. Dorin collection)

The lounge-observation area of business car No. 50 as it appeared in 1910 at the time of original construction.

(Pullman photo for EJ&E, Patrick C. Dorin collection)

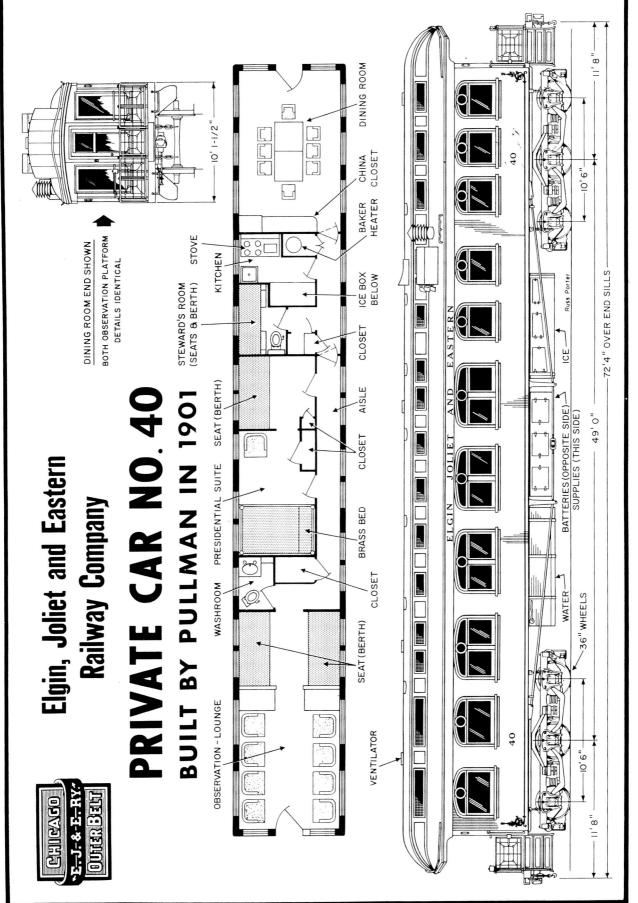

Elgin, Joliet and Eastern Railway Company

PRIVATE CAR NO. 40

BUILT BY PULLMAN IN 1901

DINING ROOM END SHOWN

BOTH OBSERVATION PLATFORM
DETAILS IDENTICAL

DINING ROOM

CHINA CLOSET

BAKER HEATER CLOSET

ICE BOX BELOW

STOVE

KITCHEN

STEWARD'S ROOM
(SEATS & BERTH)

CLOSET

AISLE

CLOSET

SEAT (BERTH)

PRESIDENTIAL SUITE

BRASS BED

CLOSET

WASHROOM

SEAT (BERTH)

OBSERVATION - LOUNGE

VENTILATOR

CHICAGO
~E~J~&~E~RY~
OuterBelt

ELGIN AND EASTERN

JOLIET

40

40

Russ Porter

ICE

BATTERIES (OPPOSITE SIDE)
SUPPLIES (THIS SIDE)

WATER

36" WHEELS

11' 8"

10' 6"

49' 0"

72' 4" OVER END SILLS

10' 6"

11' 8"

10' 1-1/2"

11' 8"

(Railroad Model Craftsman)

A drawing for business car No. 40 as built in 1901, published in *Railroad Model Craftsman* magazine in August 1965.

Interior of the dining room of business car No. 40 as built in 1901.

(Pullman photo for EJ&E, Patrick C. Dorin collection)

The lounge-observation section of car No. 40 when constructed by Pullman in 1901. *(Pullman photo for EJ&E, Patrick C. Dorin collection)*

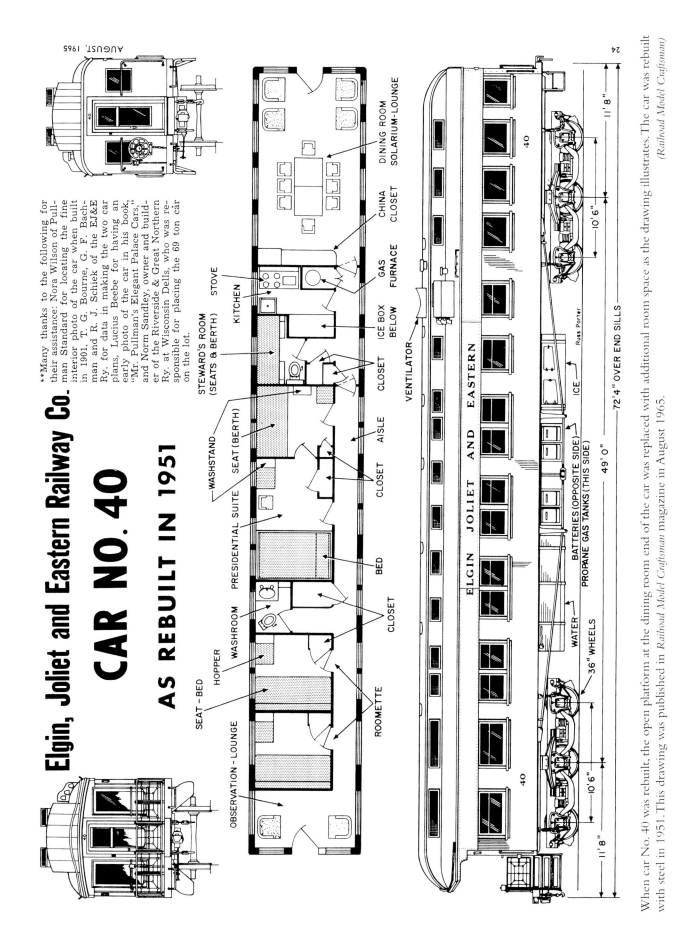

Elgin, Joliet and Eastern Railway Co.
CAR NO. 40
AS REBUILT IN 1951

AUGUST, 1965

**Many thanks to the following for their assistance: Nora Wilson of Pullman Standard for locating the fine interior photo of the car when built in 1901, T. G. Bourne, G. F. Bachman and R. J. Schiek of the EJ&E Ry. for data in making the two car plans, Lucius Beebe for having an early photo of the car in his book, "Mr. Pullman's Elegant Palace Cars," and Norm Sandley, owner and builder of the Riverside & Great Northern Ry. at Wisconsin Dells, who was responsible for placing the 69 ton car on the lot.

SEAT–BED

HOPPER

WASHROOM

PRESIDENTIAL SUITE

WASHSTAND

SEAT (BERTH)

STEWARD'S ROOM
(SEATS & BERTH)

KITCHEN

STOVE

ICE BOX
BELOW

GAS
FURNACE

CHINA
CLOSET

DINING ROOM

SOLARIUM-LOUNGE

CLOSET

AISLE

CLOSET

BED

CLOSET

ROOMETTE

OBSERVATION – LOUNGE

VENTILATOR

ELGIN JOLIET AND EASTERN

40

40

Russ Porter

ICE

24

11' 8"

10' 6"

72' 4" OVER END SILLS

BATTERIES (OPPOSITE SIDE)

PROPANE GAS TANKS (THIS SIDE)

49' 0"

WATER

36" WHEELS

10' 6"

11' 8"

When car No. 40 was rebuilt, the open platform at the dining room end of the car was replaced with additional room space as the drawing illustrates. The car was rebuilt with steel in 1951. This drawing was published in *Railroad Model Craftsman* magazine in August 1965.

(Railroad Model Craftsman)

This photo illustrates the lounge or dining room end of No. 40 after rebuilding in 1951. *(Russ Porter photo, Patrick C. Dorin collection)*

This EJ&E photo illustrates a business car train operating through part of the Gary Works steel mill complex. The ex-Milwaukee Road streamlined dining car is the second car in the train behind the steam-generator heater car; its number was 103, the same number it carried on the Milwaukee Road as part of 1937-built series 102–108. *(EJ&E)*

The EJ&E uniform for staff on the business cars.

(both, Lake Superior Railroad Museum)

One last look at business car No. 40 after being rebuilt with one open platform and modernized windows.

(EJ&E)

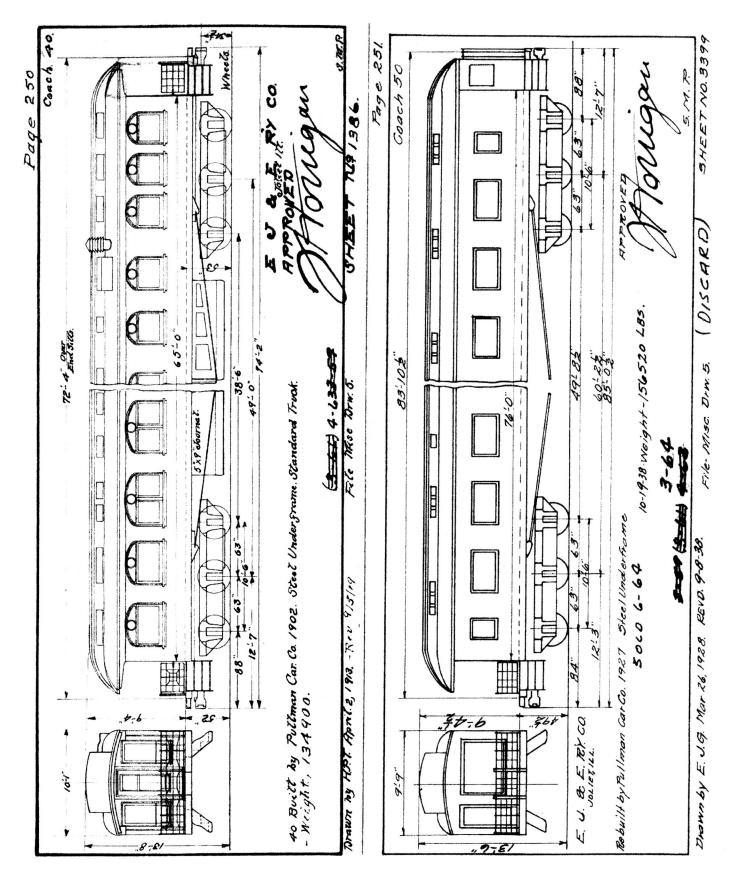

The four diagrams on these pages depict EJ&E passenger cars. *(Patrick C. Dorin collection)*

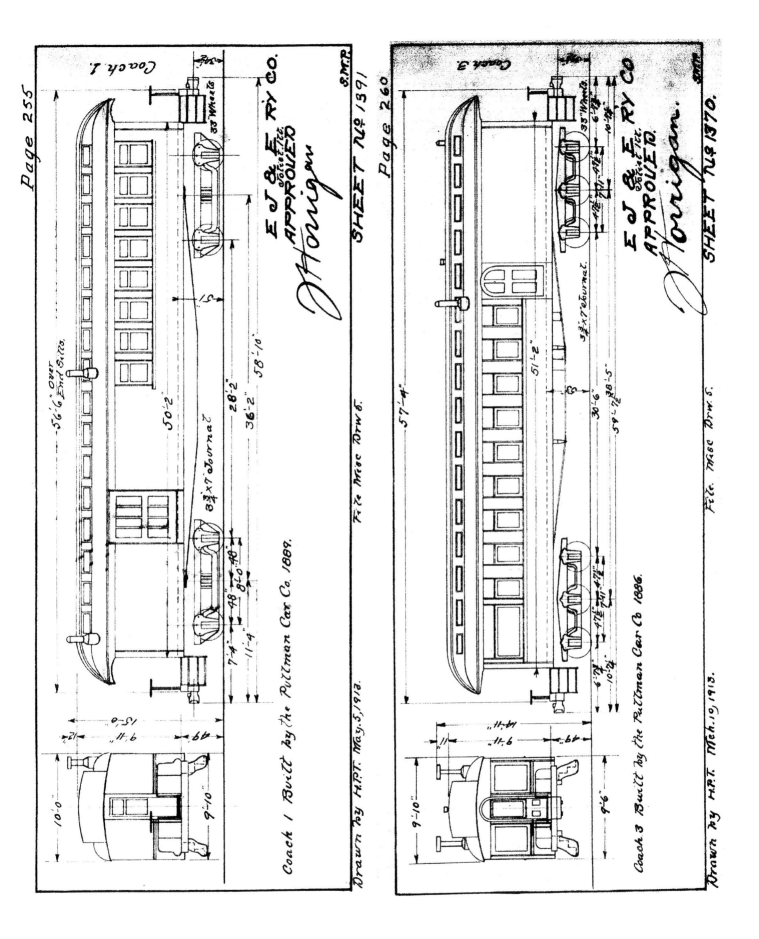

Believe It Or Not We Once Had Passenger Service

On occassion the question arises as to whether or not the "J" ever had passenger service. That question was recently answered by George Campbell of Wilmette.

Printed here is a schedule of passenger service the "J" ran in conjunction with a fair. The schedule was taken from the Lake County Independent newspaper on September 1, 1901, which was furnished by Mr. Campbell.

Special Train Service

Fair officials have succeeded in obtaining special train service during the fair over the EJ&E railroad between Libertyville and Barrington and Waukegan. The following schedule is to be in vogue, Sept. 5th and 6th between Barrington and Libertyville:

Leaves	Barrington	9:00 a.m.
"	Lake Zurich	9:15 a.m.
"	Gilmer	9:25 a.m.
"	Diamond Lake	9:35 a.m.
"	Leithton	9:40 a.m.
"	Rondout	10:00 a.m.
Arrive	Libertyville	10:15 a.m.

Between Waukegan & Libertyville

The service between Waukegan and Libertyville will be in effect three days, Sept. 4th, 5th and 6th.

Leave	Waukegan	9:40 a.m.	and 12:35 p.m.
"	N. Chicago	9:50 a.m.	and 12:45 p.m.
"	Rondout	10:00 a.m.	and 12:55 p.m.
Arrive	Libertyville	10:15 a.m.	and 1:10 p.m.

Article from the 1979 *J-Milepost* magazine, issue of January–February, Volume 32, No. 311.

Metra operates varied motive power for commuter rail service, such as No. 112 heading a 4-car train, just before rush hour, at River Grove on former Milwaukee Road trackage, now part of the Canadian Pacific/Soo Line system. No. 112 is an EMD F40PH with 3200 horsepower. This is the kind of Metra train which could operate on EJ&E in the future.   *(Patrick C. Dorin)*

- PART II -

MOTIVE POWER AND EQUIPMENT

The second part of this book is devoted to the various types of steam and diesel motive power, and the wide variety of freight and work equipment that provided the tools for the train services "Around—Not Thru Chicago."

The chapters include the types of motive power and equipment, color schemes, and other information that should be useful for rail enthusiasts and historians, providing a bit of history on the locomotives and types of cars that can provide appropriate service levels for the variety of North American shippers.

Steam power was replaced by diesel motive power by 1948. Some of the steam power lived on a bit with a transfer to the Duluth, Missabe & Iron Range Railway in northern Minnesota. The type of diesel power that made up the EJ&E fleet was purchased with the goal of providing the best power for EJ&E's wide variety of switching, transfer and over the road freight services with many interchange stops.

The freight car fleet reflected the company's predominant steel traffic base with a wide variety of hopper cars for coal, coke and cement handling; and the other equipment for steel handling including coiled steel cars, gondolas and the box car fleet. Flat cars are also an important segment of the total fleet.

Color schemes for both motive power and equipment cover the entire territory of black, light brown, orange, and orange and green with a variety of striping, lettering and insignia colors including white, yellow and green. The various photos show the different types of color applications.

Part II also contains basic information regarding the locomotive rosters and rolling stock data from the 1950s through to the time of this writing in early 2004. The rosters are not a complete listing of all freight equipment from the 1900s, which would be the subject of a complete book by itself. Additional car roster information is presented in Appendix 1.

EJ&E 0-6-0 switcher No. 37 was built by Baldwin in 1904 and was equipped with a slope-back tender for easier backup operations, and for better visibility of the yard crews. Typical of its time of construction, the locomotive has slide valves. The right side of No 37 was photographed in storage at South Chicago in May, 1938. *(Harold K. Vollrath collection)*

No. 63 illustrates the left side of one 0-6-0. Steam power carried EJ&E lettering on the cab with the "Chicago Outer Belt Line" insignia on the tenders. No. 63 was built by Alco in 1907, and was at Gary on August 31, 1937. *(Jay Williams collection)*

Chapter 7

STEAM POWER

STEAM handled the freight and switching services for the J since the company's beginning with the early predecessor railroads. The railroad operated a variety of motive power with a high percentage of switch engines. For a major portion of the steam power history, the engines carried the words "Chicago Outer Belt Line" on the tenders with the EJ&E initials on the locomotive cabs.

The J began dieselization in 1936 which was completed by the early 1950s. Some of the EJ&E steam power was sold to the Duluth, Missabe & Iron Range Railway. One of the 2-8-2 locomotives was placed on display in a park along 4th Avenue—just east of downtown—in Gary, Indiana. Chapter 8 contains an account of EJ&E diesel power.

The following tables and photographs describe and illustrate the steam locomotive throughout its history as the primary power of the EJ&E. ❏

0-6-0 No. 117 was built a bit later by Cooke in 1910. The engine was assigned to Gary, Indiana when photographed in July, 1934. The switch engines were assigned to both the Kirk Yard and the Gary Works steel mill intra–plant operations.

(Harold K. Vollrath collection)

STEAM LOCOMOTIVE ROSTER

THE FINAL DECADE 1940s

Number Series	Builder	Date	Off Roster
Type:	**0-6-0**		
27	Pittsburgh	1900	1940
31	Alco	1901	1941
34, 37, 44	Baldwin	1903	1941
46	Alco	1904	1940
50	Alco	1904	1941
53, 54	Alco	1905	1941
56, 57	Alco	1905	1941
59, 60	Alco	1905	1940-41
62, 63	Alco	1907	1940-41
65, 66	Alco	1907	1940
69-71	Alco	1906	1941-42
72 to 81	Alco	1906-07	1940-45
83 to 89	Alco	1907	1940-45
92 to 120	Alco	1910	1940-45
121	Porter	1927	1945
122	Baldwin	1917	1946

Class	Number Series	Builder	Date	Off Roster
Type: 0-8-0				
AS-1	300, 301	Baldwin	1905	1942
AS	302 to 304	Alco	1907	1945-48
	305 to 311	Alco	1910	1945-48
AS-2	312 to 320	Alco	1916	1949-50
AS-3	321 to 328	Alco	1917	1948-49
AS-4 USRA	329 to 336	Baldwin	1919	1948-50
A-2	600 to 602 Converted from 2-8-0s	Alco	1910	1945-49
Type:	**2-6-0**			
	123	Baldwin	1915	1947
Type: 2-8-0				
	528 to 530	Alco	1907	1941-42
	539 to 540	Alco	1900	1941-45
A	541 to 544	Baldwin	1903	1941-45
Type: 2-8-0				
A-1	545 to 548	Alco	1904	1940-45
A-2	549 to 599	Alco	1905-1910	1940-49
Type: 2-8-2				
AS	700 to 737	Alco	1913-18	1946-49
AS	738 to 755	Alco	1918-1923	1948
AS	756 to 760	Lima	1923	1947-48
AS	761 to 774	Baldwin	1929-30	1946-48

No. 122 was built by Baldwin in 1917, and was equipped with a larger tender. Note the piston valves in the steam cylinders as well as other enhancements of the 0-6-0 design, shown at Gary on April 29, 1937. *(R.F. Blackburn photo, Jay Williams collection)*

No. 123 was actually a 2-6-0 with a slope-back tender. The engine was built by Baldwin in 1910 and assigned to switching service. In this case, the 123 is on duty in South Chicago in July of 1930. *(Harold K. Vollrath collection)*

No. 312 was a powerful 0-8-0 switcher for heavy-duty operations on the EJ&E at Chicago, Gary and Joliet. No. 312 was built by Pittsburgh in 1917 and is shown here in operation at Gary in April, 1935. The engine has white flags flying, which may mean that the 312 is about to take a train from Gary to South Chicago. *(R.F. Blackburn photo, Jay Williams collection)*

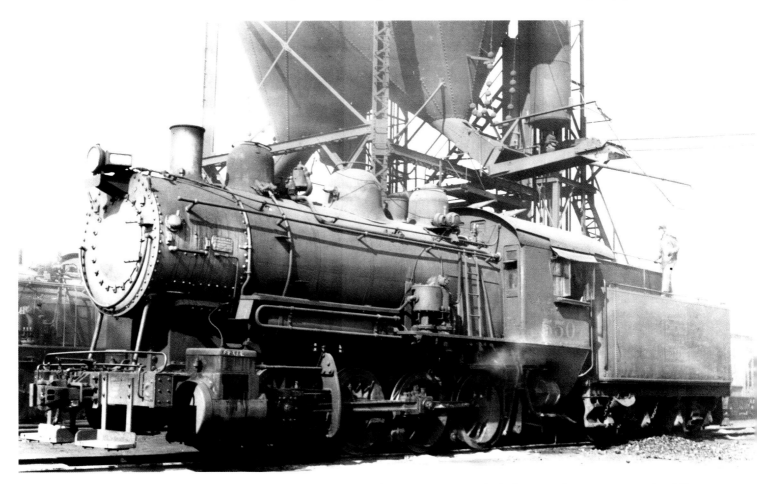

The number on this 0-8-0 is a little obscured, but appears to be 550, an engine rebuilt from an Alco 2-8-0. Note the different type of tender as compared to No. 312, shown above. It was photographed at Gary. *(R.F. Blackburn photo, Jay Williams collection)*

0-8-0 No. 559 was on assignment at Waukegan, Illinois in May, 1937 when its portrait was taken. The assignments at Waukegan were responsible for switching the yard, building trains, and pick-up and delivery service to the area shippers and receivers.

(Joseph Sleger photo, William S. Kuba Collection)

There is no doubt about it, the 571 is truly a work of art. The engine is the former 91, and was built by Pittsburgh in 1905. The 571 was assigned to the East Joliet Yard when photographed in September, 1937.

(Harold K. Vollrath collection)

No. 570 was a 2-8-0, a type assigned to freight runs and local work as well as switching and yard service. No. 570 was the former 93, which was built by Pittsburgh in 1905. The 570 is between assignments at the East Joliet Yard in August, 1928.

(Harold K. Vollrath collection)

No. 601 is still another example of the fleet of 2-8-0s in operation on the EJ&E during the steam era. With white flags on the nose, the 601 will soon be handling a freight from South Chicago to Gary in this July, 1934 photo.

(Harold K. Vollrath collection)

This is the largest and heaviest road power to be found on the EJ&E during the steam era. No. 739, a big 2-8-2, rests at Waukegan between runs on October 11, 1936.

(Joseph Sleger photo, William S. Kuba collection)

The Elgin, Joliet and Eastern Railway

Husky 2-8-2 No. 742 has had a massive feedwater heater added to the smokebox (compare No. 743, below). No. 742 was part of the 738–755 series of locomotives which were built by Alco between 1918 and 1923. *(Jay Williams collection)*

No. 743 has just taken on a load of coal and the fireman is taking a break and is looking out the window at the photographer. The Brooks-built locomotive was at Porter, Indiana on November 2, 1947. *(C. T. Felstead photo, Jay Williams collection)*

SWITCH ENGINES

Alco switcher HH 660 No. 211 was ultimately painted in the EJ&E's brown switcher color scheme with white lettering and striping. The 211 was assigned to Waukegan/North Chicago in 1962 when this photo was taken. *(Russ Porter)*

HH 660 No. 212, originally brown, was painted in the green and orange color scheme with the orange lettering, numbers and insignia on the hood when photographed at East Joliet Yard in 1962. *(Russ Porter photo, Patrick C. Dorin collection)*

THE ELGIN, JOLIET AND EASTERN RAILWAY

Chapter 8

DIESEL POWER

THE EJ&E's diesel motive power history has had an interesting diversity and multiple changes since 1936 when the first switch engine arrived. The company found diesel motive power to be very productive and effective with the types of switching operations and the over-the-road interchange services on the main line from Porter to Waukegan. Dieselization of the railroad was complete by 1948. It was one of the earliest railroads to achieve that objective.

The diesel rosters in this chapter list the different types of motive power acquired by the EJ&E over the years.

The company had a high percentage of switch engines, but with the exception of the Baldwin Sharks (model DR-4-4-1500 road motive power), the company also invested heavily in the roadswitcher concept, buying from both Alco and Baldwin.

As time went on the EJ&E began to invest in roadswitchers from Electro-Motive Division. The writer recalls hearing the first group of SD9s handling transfers from Kirk Yard to the Gary Works Steel Mill while in classes at Indiana University in downtown Gary. (The university now has a complete campus near Glen Park, and it is called Indiana University–Northwest Campus.) I wondered what was happening because in 1958, I had not seen the new SD9s. It was a pleasant surprise later to see the new orange units with the long hood as the front end, so designated similarly to the Great Northern Railway's policy.

The SD units from EMD eventually led to still other new motive power from the company, as well as second hand power from the sister railroads—the Duluth, Missabe & Iron Range, and the Bessemer & Lake Erie. Photos in this chapter show some of the power carrying the DM&IR color schemes with the EJ&E lettering and insignia.

The following rosters and photos provide a review of the EJ&E diesel electric motive power since the mid-1930s through 2003. It is an exciting picture of motive power for this important railroad: "Around – Not Thru Chicago." ❑

The EJ&E also owned and operated Baldwin VO 660s, such as the 270 illustrated here. The VO 660s were rated at 660 horsepower in the same way as the Alco HH 660s. The Baldwins worked a variety of locations throughout the EJ&E during the 1940s through the early 1960s. *(Russ Porter photo, Patrick C. Dorin collection)*

DIESEL LOCOMOTIVE ROSTER

SWITCHERS

Number Series	Type	H.P.	Builder / Date		Remarks
200–208	SW	600	EMC	1936-1937	202 & 203 rebuilt as Slugs T-3 and T-4 1954 and 57
209–212	HH 660	660	Alco	1937-1940	
213–217	S1	660	Alco	1940-1941	
220–246	SW1	600	EMD	1940-1941	
249	SW1	600	EMD	1949	Purchased in 1972
270 - 272	VO 660	660	BLW	1940-1941	270 Rebuilt to T-5 in 1964
300–307	SW1200	1200	EMD	1960	
308, 309	SW1200M	1200	EMD	1947-1953	Purchased in 1978
310–321	SW1200	1200	EMD	1964-1966	Purchased in 1986
322, 323	SW1200	1200	EMD	1964	Purchased in 1988
324	SW1200	1200	EMD	1964	
400, 401	NW1	900	EMC	1937	
402	HH 900	900	Alco	1937	Renumbered 450
402(2)	NC	900	EMC	1937	
403–407	NW2	1000	EMD	1940-1941	
408	NC	900	EMC	1937	Purchased in 1946
408 (2)	NW2	1000	EMD	1942	Purchased in 1963
409–443	NW2	1000	EMD	1947-1949	
444, 445	SW1001	1000	EMD	1971	
446–449	NW2	1000	EMD	1942-1947	Purchased in 1971-73
446 (2)	SW1001	1000	EMD		Purchased in 2000
450	HH 900	900			See 402 above
450 (2)	NW2	1000	EMD	1939	Purchased in 1974
450 (3)	NW2	1000	EMD		Purchased in 2000
451–462	S2	1000	Alco	1940-1948	
451, 452 (2)	NW2	1000	EMD	1939	Purchased in 1974
453 (2)	SW900	900	EMD	1956	Purchased in 1975
454 (2)	SW9	1200	EMD	1952	Purchased in 1975
455 (2)	NW2	1000	EMD	1949	Purchased in 1975
456, 457 (2)	SW8	800	EMD	1952	Purchased in 1976
458 (2)	NW2M	1200	EMD	1949	Purchased in 1976
459 (2)	SW1000	1000	EMD	1971	Purchased in 1989
460–462	S2	1000	Alco	1944-1949	
475–484	VO 1000	1000	BLW	1941-1944	

Still another variety of the 600-horsepower group switch engines on the J were the SW1s from Electro-Motive. Number 244 was one 27 SW1s built in 1940 and '41. These nearly identical photos show, above, No. 244 and a Baldwin switcher outside the remains of the roundhouse at Waukegan, Illinois on July 31, 1966. Many of the EJ&E switch engines were sold, with the 244 going to Northern Indiana Public Service in 1968. Below, a canvas winter-weather radiator shield decorates the nose of No. 244.

(above, Richard J. Anderson photos, William S. Kuba collection; below, Ted Schnepf collection)

The latest color scheme to be found on EJ&E switch engines is the solid green with yellow lettering, insignia and striping. SW1200s, numbers 305 and 306, are working at Kirk Yard in Gary on October 9, 2003. *(Patrick C. Dorin)*

This is what No. 306 looked like prior to the newer green color scheme. The motive power was in a light brown, more like a rust color as shown here between runs at Waukegan, Illinois in August, 1967. The 306 is coupled in multiple-unit (MU) control with a rebuilt Baldwin center cab for through freight train operations between East Joliet and Waukegan. *(Harold K. Vollrath collection)*

SW1200 No. 316 displays the new green scheme applied to the rear section of the switch engine group. The 316 is between assignments and laying over at the engine facility at East Joliet in October, 2003. *(Patrick C. Dorin)*

SW1000 No. 459, which was purchased in 1989, displays the paint scheme toward the front of the locomotive, at Kirk Yard in October 2003. The new EJ&E green is now the standard application for switch engines. *(Patrick C. Dorin)*

DIESEL LOCOMOTIVE ROSTER *(continued)*

THE BALDWIN CENTER CAB FLEET

The Baldwin center cab locomotive, 2000 horsepower, played a major role in both transfer service and over the road train operations for the EJ&E. With the exception of No. 100, built in 1946, and No. 126, constructed in 1950, all of the units were built in 1948. Virtually all of the motive power was rebuilt during its operating career on the EJ&E with the exception of Numbers 100 and 118. The following table lists the unit numbers, rebuilding with either Baldwin or EMD engines, and their new number. The EMD rebuilds went into the 900 series, while the Baldwin rebuilds were renumbered in the 700s.

DT-6-6-2000

Number Series	Rebuilt With EMD / BLW Power	Date	New Number	Year Off Roster
100	None		None	1961
101, 102	Baldwin	1957, 1961	701, 702	1970
103	EMD	1956	903	1975
104, 105	Baldwin	1957, 1961	704, 705	1970, 1967
106	EMD	1956	906	1974
107	Baldwin	1958	707	1967
108	Baldwin	1957	708	1966
109, 110	EMD	1956	909, 910	1975
111	Baldwin	1961	711	1970
112–116	EMD	1956	912–916	1969–1975
117	Baldwin	1958	717	1970
118	None			1966
119	EMD	1956	919	1975
120, 121	EMD	1956	920, 921	1975, 1976
122, 123	Baldwin	1958	722, 723	1971, 1966
124, 125	EMD	1956	924, 925	1975
126	Baldwin	1958	726	1970

BALDWIN SHARK-NOSE MOTIVE POWER

700A, 701A	Cab units, purchased in 1950, off roster in 1955
700B, 701B	Booster units, purchased in 1950, off roster in 1955

ROADSWITCHERS

Number Series	Type	H.P.	Builder/Date		Remarks
500, 501	DRS-6-6-1500	1500	BLW	1949	Purchased in 1956
600–602	SD9	1750	EMD	1957	
603–613	SD9	1750	EMD	1956	Ex-DM&IR, 1959 Purchased 1968–1971
614	SD9	1750	EMD	1959	Purchased in 1997
615, 616	SD18	1800	EMD	1960	
650–655	SD38	2000	EMD	1970	
656–669	SD38-2	2000	EMD	1974–1975	

(Note: No. 658 traded to Bessemer and Lake Erie for No. 669.)

Number Series	Type	H.P.	Builder/Date		Remarks
670–675	SD38-2	2000	EMD		Purchased in 2002
700–704	GP38-2	2000	EMD	1972–1973	

(No. 703 was the only GP38-2 on the J in 2003.)

Number Series	Type	H.P.	Builder/Date		Remarks
750–752	SD40U	3000	EMD	1969–1970	
800–809	RS-2	1500	Alco	1948–1949	
802 (2)	SDM	1750	EMD	1959	
804 (2)	SD9M	1750	EMD	1959	
809 (2)	SD18M	1800	EMD	1960	Purchased in 1993
811, 813	SD18M	1800	EMD	1960	Purchased in 1997 & 1993
814, 815	SD9M	1750	EMD	1979	Purchased in 1993, 1997
818	SD18U	1800	EMD	1959	Purchased in 1998
820	SD18U	1800	EMD	1960	Purchased in 1997
851	SD18M	1800	EMD	1962	Purchased in 1995
852	SD18	1800	EMD	1962	Purchased in 1995
891	SD38-2	2000	EMD	1975	Purchased in 1986

SWITCHER BOOSTER UNITS / SLUGS

T1   Rebuilt from an Alco HH 660s and purchased in 1951.
T2

T1 (2)   Rebuilt from an Alco S locomotive.
T2 (2)   Also rebuilt from an Alco S and purchased in 2000.

T3   Rebuilt from No. 202 in 1954.
T4   Rebuilt from No. 203 in 1957.
T5   Rebuilt from No. 270 in 1964.

The 322, an SW1200, displays the paint application on the right side of the unit. The 322 and crew is working the yard at East Joliet on this cloudy afternoon in October, 2003.

(Patrick C. Dorin)

NW2 No. 417 shows the style of Roman lettering and numbers on the light brown paint scheme as applied to switch engines for many years. Note the safety stripe applications on the frame of the 417. No. 417 was being serviced at the Kirk Yard roundhouse when photographed on an early fall day in September, 1976.

(William S. Kuba)

The SW1001 switch engines can also operated as MU power for both yard and transfer assignments. The new 444 and 445 are teamed up here in October 2003 at Kirk Yard and are being readied for some heavy-duty yard work with loads of coiled steel.

(Patrick C. Dorin)

Roster shot of the SW1001's left side in the green color scheme.

(Patrick C. Dorin)

NW2 No. 434 illustrates a yellow nose with some minor striping, in a photo taken at Kirk Yard in August, 1987. Striping was also applied to the pilot. There are some interesting details regarding the 434 and the 440 to the rear. Note the underbody and the trucks are painted silver. The front center cab windows of the 434 have been blanked out, while they were retained on the 440. Another interesting twist are the rotating lights on both sides of the cab roofs of the switch engines. This was a typical application on many types of motive power on the J.

(Frank Schnick)

This photo of NW2 No. 436 clearly displays the yellow end for improved safety and visibility. The NW2 was the largest group of switch engines on the EJ&E with the series running from 403 to 443 and 446 to 452. The 436 here is on the ready track for new assignments on a nice summer day in July, 1980.

(William S. Kuba)

THE ELGIN, JOLIET AND EASTERN RAILWAY

No. 457, an SW8, was the last of eight switch engines rebuilt by Industrial Maintenance Service between 1974 and 1976. The 457 was in storage when photographed at Kirk Yard on September 23, 1976. Before rebuilding, this particular unit was Norfolk and Western No. 2109, and originally Nickel Plate Road No. 109. *(William S. Kuba)*

Shifting back a bit to 1987, these SW1200s were in the light brown scheme. However, the lettering and numbering was changed to Gothic style as illustrated with the MU-control units 320 and 315 in transfer service at Kirk Yard. On this day in August, 1987, the pair had been handling finished steel car loads from the various plant sites at U.S. Steel in Gary to the classification trackage at Kirk Yard. *(Patrick C. Dorin)*

This roster photo of the VO 1000, No. 477 was taken at the round house at Waukegan. The color scheme on the Baldwins during the 1950s and 60s was the light brown, EJ&E's standard scheme for switchers.   *(Russ Porter)*

It is July, 1966, and Baldwin VO 1000 No. 479 has been assigned for yard service at Waukegan. During the 1960s, Waukegan was the northern terminal for a total of ten freight trains per day, five arrivals and five departures. One pair, the local trains 17 and 18, were Daily Except Sunday operations. Thus, the 479 had its work cut out for it.   *(Harold K. Vollrath collection)*

A right side view of VO 1000 No. 481 at East Joliet in 1963.

(Russ Porter)

Still another view of a Baldwin VO 1000, in this photo, No. 484 which was assigned to yard duties at East Joliet in 1964.

(Russ Porter)

BALDWIN CENTER CAB FLEET

The EJ&E invested heavily in the Baldwin center cabs (Baldwin model DT-6-6-1000/2: two 1000-horsepower engines) for freight train operations over the entire main line, as well as transfer work on the South Chicago line and elsewhere. Rated at 2000 horsepower, they were among the most powerful freight motive power in production during the late 1940s. The No. 101 is shown here at Waukegan in June, 1953. At left on the Waukegan service track is No. 210, an Alco HH 660 switch engine. The 101 was later rebuilt with new Baldwin engines and renumbered into the 700 series as No. 701.　　*(Russ Porter photo, William S. Kuba collection)*

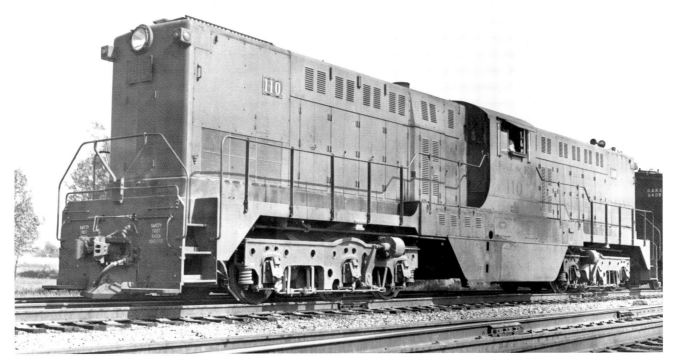

No. 110 in the full orange color scheme is heading up a freight train at Spaulding, Illinois in May, 1951. Spaulding was the Milwaukee Road connection on the west side of Chicago.

(Harold K. Vollrath collection)

EJ&E's No. 723 exhibits the orange and green color scheme which was typical in the 1950s and '60s. The 723 is shown here between runs at East Joliet in 1963. *(Russ Porter photo, Patrick C. Dorin collection)*

The 726, a Baldwin rebuild, has just dropped off a freight car for the Grand Trunk Western interchange at Griffith, Indiana, and is hurrying back to pick up its eastbound freight, No. 4, bound for Porter, Indiana. The date is September 7, 1963. *(William S. Kuba)*

No. 903 is an EMD rebuild renumbered from 103. It is in MU control with the switch engine No. 301 at Waukegan. No. 903 clearly displays the green and orange scheme, which impressed many people as being very artistic. *(Harold K. Vollrath collection)*

Rebuilt by EMD, Center Cab No. 910 is MU'd with an EMD SD9 (number not visible behind the pole), crossing the Milwaukee Road double-track main line at Rondout, Illinois in August, 1969. This was an important interchange point with the Milwaukee Road, which now (2003) is the Soo Line/Canadian Pacific. As a side note: the Milwaukee Road mainline trackage once had signs for trains approaching Rondout that instructed passenger train engineers to slow to 100 miles per hour for the crossing.

(Russ Porter photo, Patrick C. Dorin collection)

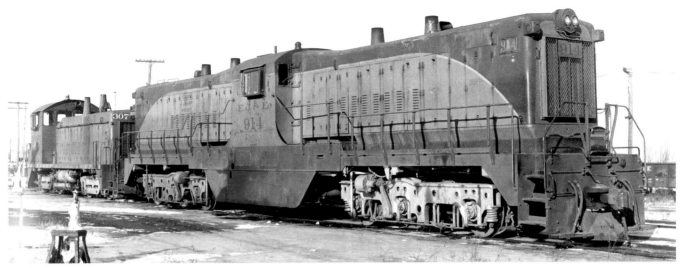

Still another view of an EMD rebuild, No. 914 MU'd with switcher No. 307. The 914 had silver-painted trucks.

(Glenn F. Monhart photo, Anthony Thompson collection)

Rebuild No. 925 retained its full orange color scheme including silver trucks. The 925 is between trips at the East Joliet engine terminal in the company of No. 906 to the left, and the VO 1000 No. 475 to the right. It is July 5, 1973.   *(William S. Kuba)*

Locomotive 925 carried the orange and green color scheme at Waukegan in November 1965.   *(Ted Schnepf collection)*

Elgin, Joliet & Eastern No. 912 shoves an SP flat car loaded with a large Caterpillar dump truck at Griffith, Indiana in May, 1964. This load is being transferred to the Erie Lackawanna. *(Emery Gulash photo, Alan Turner collection)*

BALDWIN SHARK NOSE

The EJ&E Baldwin Shark Nose covered wagon units, bought as demonstrators, had a short career on the railroad, being soon resold to Baltimore & Ohio. With the variety of interchange stops and switching, the roadswitcher type of motive power was more appropriate. Nevertheless, the four units (two A units, two B units, numbered 700A and 701A, and 700B and 701B) were artistic pieces of motive power. Note the green and orange color scheme with the EJ&E insignia on the nose. One can only imagine what EMD F units or Alco FAs may have looked like with the orange and green. *(J. Michael Gruber collection)*

ROAD SWITCHERS

Baldwin road switchers, DRS-6-6-1500, Numbers 500 and 501, were purchased from the Bessemer and Lake Erie Railroad, still another sister railroad to the EJ&E. The J acquired the two units in 1956. The units for awhile carried the B&LE color scheme with the EJ&E lettering. Later the units received the full orange color scheme. This would not be the last time that such color applications would take place. The reader will note still other road switchers later in this chapter with the DM&IR colors. The 501 is working the north end of the East Joliet Yard on June 10, 1969. *(William S. Kuba collection)*

The first EJ&E SD9s were purchased new from EMD, such as the 601 and 600 shown here. The first units were built with the long hood as the front end. (The author remembers hearing the new SD9s working transfers between Kirk Yard and the Gary Works during classes in the evenings at Indiana University in Gary. I wondered what railroad I was hearing, as I knew the J did not own such units yet—or so I thought.) The 601 and 600 are shown here at Kirk Yard in August, 1987. *(Frank Schnick)*

It is a cloudy day in August, 1987, and this ex-DM&IR SD9, now EJ&E No. 606, with the short hood as the front and equipped with dynamic brakes, rests between transfer operations at Kirk Yard.

(Patrick C. Dorin)

The 608 is another SD9 from the DM&IR fleet, in fact, the former DM&IR 135. The ex-DM&IR SD9s were also equipped with a bell over the short hood, and painted in the full orange color scheme. Only the letters EJ&E and number were applied to the sides of the cab.

(William S. Kuba)

SD18 No. 616 is a former DM&IR unit and still carries DM&IR paint, but with the addition of EJ&E lettering and insignia. With the J insignia on the short hood, the paint scheme seems almost perfectly natural for its new ownership since the DM&IR was once a sister railroad to the EJ&E. The 616 is working the hump at Kirk Yard in this October, 2003 photo.   *(Patrick C. Dorin)*

SD38 No. 653 is shown arriving at Porter, Indiana with a short freight on a snowy day back in the early 1970s. Note the depth of the snow which was a bit unusual for northwestern Indiana. The 653 has coupled up to the caboose to lay over until time to make the return trip to East Joliet.

(Frank Schnick)

The EJ&E invested in a grand total of 17 SD38s and SD38-2s. No. 664 was still new on the property when it was placed in storage at Gary, Indiana in September, 1976 during a business slowdown. The 664 had been delivered to the J in January, 1975. This locomotive has the full orange color scheme with the silver underframe and trucks. *(William S. Kuba)*

SD38-2 No. 658 displays the orange color scheme with a number of refinements. Note the J insignia on the long hood, and the white safety stripes at the rear of the unit. The 658 was laying over at East Joliet in this October 2003 photo. *(Patrick C. Dorin)*

No. 665 displays the safety stripes on the nose of the nose of the SD38-2s. The 665 is keeping company with Union Pacific motive power from a coal train at East Joliet on October 9, 2003.   *(Patrick C. Dorin)*

SD38-2 No. 667 laying over at Kirk Yard. One cab door is open.   *(Patrick C. Dorin)*

The 670 illustrates the application of the safety stripes on the side of the SD38-2s. The unit is laying over at Kirk Yard.

(Patrick C. Dorin)

The EJ&E also invested in a small fleet of GP38-2s, number series 700–704. At first the units were dressed in the full orange color scheme with silver trucks and underframe. The units originally were equipped with two rotating lights on each side of the cab roof. The GP38-2s were operated in all types of service including yard switching, transfers and road freights.

(William S. Kuba)

No. 800 was the first of the RS-2s purchased by the EJ&E; it is shown here working the yard at East Joliet in the vivid all-orange color scheme.
(Russ Porter photo, Patrick C. Dorin collection)

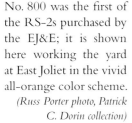

The EJ&E invested in a fleet of ten RS-2s from Alco in 1948–1949. The units were painted in the full orange scheme as described previously. By the early 1970s, the RS-2s were no longer on the roster. In this September, 1969 photo, No. 802 is in road service with a train at Griffith, Indiana with a cab-side spill. The RS-2s served in a variety of assignments over the years. The author recalls seeing the RS-2s on a daily basis on the evening run over the short branch line from the west end of Kirk Yard to the east side of Gary to serve a variety of industries.

(William S. Kuba)

THE ELGIN, JOLIET AND EASTERN RAILWAY

The EJ&E ultimately had two sets of 800-series motive power. No. 804 is a former DM&IR SD9M, which is working the hump at Kirk Yard in October, 2003. The EJ&E lettering on the rear section of the arrow was painted on in white as were the numbers in the arrowhead.   *(Patrick C. Dorin)*

SD9M No. 814 had the numbers and EJ&E initials painted on using the maroon color of the DM&IR. Note the J insignia on the side of the nose in this view at Kirk Yard, October, 2003.   *(Patrick C. Dorin)*

No. 852 is a SD18 with a low nose and complete orange color scheme. The insignias are applied in green on the long hood as well as on the nose. Kirk yard, October, 2003. *(Patrick C. Dorin)*

GP38-2 No. 703 in the "The J" color scheme with the symbol on the nose and on the sides of the long hood. *(EJ&E)*

Switcher Booster Units / Slugs

The slug units are generally coupled up and MU'd with switch engines. The EJ&E owned and operated as many as seven slugs over the past several decades. The current slug T1 was rebuilt from an Alco switch engine, and is the second slug numbered T1. The T1 was in service at Kirk Yard when its portrait was taken in October, 2003.

(Patrick C. Dorin)

This slug T2 is the second unit numbered T2. It was also rebuilt from an Alco switch engine and purchased by the EJ&E in the year 2000. The current T1 and T2 are painted in the green color scheme with yellow striping. When photographed at the East Joliet engine terminal in October 2003, the T2 was MU'd with switcher 450, which carries the green scheme with new yellow striping on the hood.

(Patrick C. Dorin)

Slug T5, shown here at Kirk Yard, was rebuilt from one of the J's switch engines, No. 270, in 1964. The T5 was painted in the light brown paint scheme when its portrait was taken in August, 1987.

(Frank Schnick)

This 40-ton double wood sheathed box car of United States Railway Administration design was built by American Car & Foundry in August of 1919, one of 500 cars in the series 7300–7799. The suffix "C.T." on the car number indicates that it was owned not by the EJ&E itself but by the Columbia Trust, an agency created by the federal government to finance USRA freight cars when the railroads to which they were assigned could not afford outright purchase.   *(AC&F photo, Al Westerfield collection)*

The EJ&E rebuilt its USRA wood sheathed box cars in 1936-1937 with new all steel bodies, re-using the original underframes, trucks, and ends, but applying new sides, Creco three-panel doors, Murphy rectangular panel steel roofs, Universal geared hand brakes, and AB air brake equipment. In the process, their capacity was increased to 3250 cubic feet. This car is shown in the early 1950s paint and lettering with the "Around – Not Thru Chicago" map.   *(Tom Klinger collection)*

Chapter 9

THE BOX CAR FLEET

THE box car fleet is one of the most prominent pieces of equipment to be found on any railroad. The size and the colors as well as the various slogans are quite noticeable on a box car. The box car group during the 1940s through the 1970s were painted with a variety of colors. Some were painted a solid green, while others wore a two-tone green and orange scheme. A complete map of the railroad graced the upper right hand corner of many of the EJ&E box cars. Since the 1960s, the box cars have been largely painted with a solid orange with different styles of lettering, numbers and insignias. This chapter is a pictorial review of the many types of box cars owned and operated by the EJ&E including a photograph of a relatively unknown part of the fleet. Yes, believe it or not, the EJ&E once even leased a small fleet of refrigerator cars. ❏

The first all-steel box cars built new for the EJ&E were five hundred cars in the 60400–60899 series delivered by American Car & Foundry's Chicago plant in the summer of 1941. As shown here, they were basically of 40-foot, 6-inch AAR alternate standard design with 10-foot, 6-inch inside height, 5-5 Dreadnaught ends, and Murphy rectangular panel steel roofs, but had full-length center-reinforced side sills and 8-foot door openings, with Superior 7-panel doors. Running boards were steel grid and trucks were AAR with spring planks and Barber lateral-motion bolsters. *(George Sisk photo, Charles Winters collection)*

Another five hundred 40-foot, 6-inch steel box cars in the 60900–61399 series joined the EJ&E roster in 1948. Though they resembled their prewar predecessors, they were different in numerous details. Doors were still 8-foot wide Superior 7-panel design, and roofs were Murphy rectangular panel with steel grid running boards, but inside height was lower at 10 feet, and sides were twelve-panel instead of ten-panel, with notched side sills. Ends were of postwar 3½ /4 rib Improved Dreadnaught design and trucks were ASF A-3 "Ride Control."   *(John C. LaRue, Jr. collection)*

The 60934 provides another view of the 60900–61399 series. These cars were solid green in color with orange lettering and map. The car was on the Southern Pacific at Colton, California on January 8, 1955.   *(Chet McCoid photo, Bob's Photo collection)*

Box car 61155 takes us into the late 1950s, with a different lettering arrangement as compared to cars 61026 and 60934. The EJ&E emblem in the form of initials is now in 4-foot lettering and the map has fallen out of use.   *(Jay Williams collection)*

As time went on the EJ&E fleet advanced from solid green colors for the box car fleet to an orange and green color combination. Car 61226 (series 60900–61399) was built in 1948 and received the new colors in the mid-1950s. The lettering in the orange band is green while the lettering in the green area is in the orange. Note the style of the 8-foot Superior door on this group of cars. The car was photographed at Readville Yard, Boston, on September 28, 1957.   *(Chet McCoid photo, Bob's Photo collection)*

This color view vividly depicts the lettering scheme, though the car details are not as well shown in the shadows. The photo was taken at Los Angeles in July 1961.

(Morris Abowitz photo, Bill Sheehan collection)

The year 1964 brought the arrival of a fleet of 54-foot, 6-inch box cars with 10-foot single doors and 70-ton capacity. Car 62020 was painted in the full orange scheme with the green lettering, numbers, and insignia; its number series was 62000–62074.

(Jay Williams collection)

Car 62069 from the 62000–62074 series had been freshly repainted with the orange color scheme and carried the current "J" insignia. Running boards have been removed. The car was photographed at East Joliet Yard in October, 2003.   *(Patrick C. Dorin)*

These EJ&E box cars have orange sides and green lettering, and black ends with white lettering. They were photographed in a Milwaukee Road train near Milwaukee; they are from the 63000-63074 series of 50-foot, 6-inch box cars with cushion underframes. Note EJ&E gondola 34527 to the right of the photo. *(Russ Porter)*

Box car 65022's portrait was taken in Duluth, Minnesota in the former downtown Northern Pacific freight yard. The number series 65000–65179 was painted all-orange color with green lettering. Note that doors are not the same width. *(Patrick C. Dorin)*

In the 1950s, EJ&E was still leasing refrigerator cars from General American (compare photo below), with GARX 4505 shown in service at Tampa, Florida. *(K.B. King photo, Richard Buike collection)*

The EJ&E leased some refrigerator cars during the 1930s from General American, with the reporting marks GARX. Car 9995 was photographed in Buffalo, New York in 1938. It is not known what the exact colors were, but note the EJ&E's Chicago Outer Belt line insignia during that period of time.

(Harold K. Vollrath collection)

The Standard Steel Car Company built five hundred 46-foot composite mill gondolas of 70-ton capacity for the EJ&E in 1923, numbered 80000–80499. This builder's portrait shows EJ&E 80100 when new. Stout fishbelly center and side sills supported body framing consisting of hat section vertical posts and channel section diagonals. These cars had fixed ends of 5-rib corrugated steel, ARA cast steel trucks with Simplex lateral motion bolsters, top-operated Type D couplers with Carmer uncoupling levers, and lever and ratchet style hand brakes. *(Standard Steel Car Company photo, Tom Martorano collection)*

In 1939 and 1940, the EJ&E rebuilt its 80000-series gondolas with steel sides replacing their original wood side sheathing, but retaining the steel framing. In this form, they lasted through World War II and well into the 1950s. Here is freshly painted EJ&E 80047 as it appeared at Fort Bragg, North Carolina in January of 1952. Stenciling on the side sill indicates that by that time it had been equipped with AB air brake equipment and wrought steel wheels. *(Chet McCoid photo, Bob's Photo collection)*

In 1929 the EJ&E purchased 250 mill gondolas in the 80500–80749 series from American Car & Foundry. These 70-ton cars were 48 feet, 6 inches long inside and were of all-steel construction except for wood floors. They had fishbelly center sills but their side sills were straight; ends were three-rib Dreadnaught and trucks were Dalman two-level design with Barber lateral motion bolsters. EJ&E 80553 was at East St. Louis, Illinois in 1936. *(Joe Collias collection)*

Chapter 10

GONDOLAS AND CARS FOR COILED STEEL

THE gondola and coiled steel car fleet was (and is) primarily devoted to the steel company freight traffic with a variety of products from Gary, Indiana and elsewhere on the EJ&E system. Most of the cars were painted black with white lettering. Some of the coiled steel cars were also black with orange covers. The gondola fleet included cars from 40 feet long to 65 feet (and longer) inside length, with a variety of low sides and high side equipment.

A number of the gondolas were also equipped with troughs for handling coiled steel. In addition to the extensive gondola fleet, purpose-built coil cars with hoods were also included in the roster. And part of the fleet also included covered gondolas for weather protection for a variety of sensitive steel products. The cars added a significant amount of diversity to EJ&E freight car fleet designed to meet specific shipper and receiver needs. ❏

The EJ&E owned and operated a fairly large fleet of low-side gondolas for a variety of services, of which the 80500–80749 series is an example. Car 80551, little changed after more than thirty years in service, was at Hamlet, North Carolina in March 1960. The only modifications to the car were the application of AB air brakes, wrought steel wheels, and later style stenciling. Open journal box lids indicate that journal oil was in the process of being added. *(Chet McCoid photo, Bob's Photo collection)*

E.J. & E. 3-47 ST. L.
A. C. & F. CO. LOT 2968
Negative #180384-A-2

The EJ&E ordered 550 additional 48-foot, 6-inch all-steel mill gondolas from the Mt. Vernon Car Manufacturing Company in 1937 which, though similar to the 1929 cars, were of only 50 tons capacity. Numbered in the 31000–31549 series, these cars had straight rolled steel center sills, steel floors, and inverse Dreadnaught drop ends. Their construction saved over 6,000 pounds owing to the use of Cor-Ten and Man-Ten alloy steels, proprietary compositions of EJ&E owner United States Steel, which publicized the cars widely as examples of the weight saving attainable with these alloys. Several additional orders were placed for cars of this design, culminating in 1947 with the 34200–34899 series built by American Car & Foundry, as shown in this builder's portrait.

(American Car & Foundry photo, Hawkins-Wider-Long collection)

One group of EJ&E 48-foot, 6-inch mill gondolas differed significantly from the others. When the 33250–34189 series were built in late 1942, sheet steel was in critically short supply owing to wartime shortages, so these cars had wood side sheathing and floors and incorporated diagonal braces in their side framing. Here is a builder's photo of EJ&E 33327 showing its original composite construction.

(American Car & Foundry photo, Hawkins-Wider-Long collection)

This is what the wartime composite cars looked like after they were rebuilt with new fishbelly sides and steel floors, which EJ&E did in the late 1940s to create all-steel cars. The cars remained 49 feet long inside. EJ&E 33547 was at San Diego in February 1957.

(Chet McCoid photo, Bob's Photo collection)

Another lettering style on the rebuilt wartime gondolas is shown on car 33282 (33250–33749 series), upgraded by now to 55-ton capacity (originally 50 tons). The car was at Potomac Yard, Washington, DC, in August 1968.

(Chet McCoid photo, Bob's Photo collection)

EJ&E 34921 (from series 34900–35399) is a 48-foot, 6-inch low-side car upgraded to 55-ton capacity, though built in 1952 as a 50-ton car. It was photographed at Potomac Yard in Washington, DC in May 1968. The lettering style with insignia was a work of art and brought attention to the EJ&E as an important railroad.

(Chet McCoid photo, Bob's Photo collection)

Like all the cars in its series (34900–35399), gondola 35055 had a wooden floor and had an inside height of just 3 feet. The car carried a simpler lettering scheme with the basic reporting marks, typical of later days.

(Patrick C. Dorin)

Like other railroads that served the steel industry, the EJ&E found itself needing longer mill gondolas than the 48-foot, 6-inch cars it then had in service and purchased in 1937 a hundred cars of 70 tons capacity and 65 feet inside length. The 90000–90099 series had steel floors, reverse Dreadnaught drop ends, and were unusually narrow to avoid excessive center overhang owing to their long wheelbase. When EJ&E 90062 was photographed about 1960, it was stenciled "WHEN EMPTY RETURN TO EJ&E RY. SO. CHICAGO IL."

(Paul Dunn photo, Richard Burg collection)

Another example of the long mill gondolas is No. 90673, part of the 90600–90699 series built in 1969. The series is 66 feet long inside with a 70-ton capacity. The car was equipped with permanent blocking equipment for loading of steel products when photographed at Potomac Yard in October 1969.

(Bob's Photo collection)

In the 1960s, EJ&E began to acquire 100-ton cars. Gondola 4548 (originally from series 4500–4584) was 49 feet long inside, with a 100-ton capacity. Note the white panel at the left end of the car, which contains a notice that the car is equipped for coil steel loading. Photographed at Kirk Yard during the summer of 1987.

(Frank Schnick)

Car 4642 (series 4635–4664) was a 51-foot, 11-inch car with a cushion underframe, roof, and troughs for coiled steel traffic. As with most EJ&E gondolas, the car was painted black with white lettering. *(Patrick C. Dorin)*

In November 1980, ACF Industries built 150 cars for a 100-ton gondola series, numbered 87000–88149. Here we see car 87936 as an example; these cars were 52 feet, 6 inches long inside. *(Frank Schnick)*

Car 87974 from the same series, 87000–88149, gives us a good look at its very slender style of lettering. Again, this car was lettered only with the reporting marks and dimensional data. *(Patrick C. Dorin)*

Car 88874, from 100-ton series 88500–88899 was another gondola with EJ&E's virtually standard 52 feet, 6-inch interior length. Note that the superstructure was entirely of riveted construction. *(Frank Schnick)*

Car 4289 was a 52-foot, 6-inch car with a 100-ton capacity, part of the 4200–4349 series, built in the late 1970s. The car was assigned to coil steel service, as denoted by its white end panel. It was photographed at the Kirk Yard hump in October 2003. *(Patrick C. Dorin)*

Gondola 4416 (4410–4549 series) is yet another of EJ&E's many 52-foot, 6-inch cars for coil steel service, and is so loaded in this view at Kirk Yard in October 2003. It has the usual white panel for coil service at the left end of the car, and has the modern "J" insignia at car center. *(Patrick C. Dorin)*

Rusty gondola 88857 (88500–88899 series) is another coil steel car, 52 feet, 6 inches long inside and with a 4-foot, 6-inch inside height. In this photograph at Kirk Yard in October 2003, it carries three large steel coils set flat on the car floor. *(Patrick C. Dorin)*

Gondola 90666 (90600–90699 series) is a long mill gondola, 66 feet long inside and with a 5-foot, 6-inch inside height (most EJ&E long mill gondolas had 3-foot, 6-inch inside height); it was photographed in October 2003. *(Patrick C. Dorin)*

Built in September 1980 by the Thrall Car Company, 52-foot, 6-inch gondola 88330 was part of the 88300–88399 series. These nominally 100-ton cars had welded superstructures with an unusual rib at the bottom of the side stakes. *(Patrick C. Dorin)*

Gondola 3834 (3800–3891 series) is equipped with a cushion underframe and round-top covers for coiled steel service, shown at East Joliet in October 2003. *(Patrick C. Dorin)*

Purpose-built coil steel car 7340 was part of the 7300–7349 series when built. As one would guess, the cars operated exclusively for coiled steel products. This car with angled covers was at Kirk Yard during August 1987. *(Frank Schnick)*

THE ELGIN, JOLIET AND EASTERN RAILWAY

EJ&E purpose-built coil steel car 6937 (6850–6949 series) is equipped with two round-top covers. The car color scheme is black for the car itself, and orange for the covers. It was at Kirk Yard, October 2003. *(Patrick C. Dorin)*

Car 7213 from the 7100–7238 series was also equipped with round-top covers at Kirk Yard in October 2003. *(Patrick C. Dorin)*

Coil steel car 7638 (7500–7699 series) is equipped with a single round-top cover extending the full length of the 52-foot, 7-inch car (only 42 feet inside). It was photographed at Kirk Yard in October 2003. The color scheme is black for the car body, and a brown or olive color for the cover. *(Patrick C. Dorin)*

In 1940 the EJ&E purchased 50 covered hoppers from American Car & Foundry for bulk cement loading. These 70-ton cars, numbered 3000–3049, were an early design with ten roof hatches and a capacity of only 1790 cubic feet.
(AC&F photo, Hawkins-Wider-Long collection)

Car 3063 was part of the 3050–3099 series, built in 1946 with a 70-ton capacity. This was the most common type of late 1940s covered hopper when built in 1949, with square roof hatches, though the EJ&E cars had equally spaced hatches, unlike the cars purchased by most railroads. The car was at Joliet on October 19, 1952.
(Chet McCoid photo, Bob's Photo collection)

Car 3310 was part of the 70-ton 3200–3399 series. Note the channel rib at each bolster on the car side and round loading hatches on the roof. This car is a Pullman-Standard PS-2 covered hopper design, produced in the thousands for many railroads and other buyers. When photographed at Omaha, Nebraska on June 7, 1963, the paint scheme was gray with black lettering including two small emblems: the full EJ&E at the far right, and the "Around–Not Thru Chicago" on the far left.
(J. Michael Gruber collection)

Chapter 11

HOPPER, BALLAST AND FLAT CARS

THE EJ&E hopper car fleet, including the ballast cars, is a very interesting group. The company owned and operated 50-ton equipment with two hopper doors, both the offset side (inside post) and the rib side (outside post) varieties. The fleet extended through 70-ton cars plus the large cubic capacity coke cars.

Coal traffic on the EJ&E once included delivery of coal to various coal yards along the entire system for home heating. Other forms of traffic included electric generating plants plus coal for the coke plants at Gary and Joliet. Once the coal was proessed into coke, it was transported in the high cubic capacity cars to the iron- and steelmaking furnaces in South Chicago and Gary Works.

In the 21st century, coal hauling equipment on the EJ&E continues to come from a variety of mining areas for both metallurgical and energy producers. Thus one can see equipment with BN, BNSF, UP, NS, Conrail, CSXT and other reporting marks. Although not owned by or part of the EJ&E fleet, they have added to the variety of equipment observed on the EJ&E.

Coal hopper cars are not the only part of the fleet. The railroad also owns and operates a fleet of covered hopper cars. Most of this equipment was painted in the typical grey color schemes with the black lettering, much of which operated for cement traffic.

BALLAST CARS. Still another group of equipment within this category are the ballast cars. Although often thought of as "work cars" the ballast cars are often operated in stone service and interchange with other railroads. The

EJ&E has a variety of ballast cars, part of which are ore cars from the Duluth, Missabe & Iron Range Railway. The cars have retained their yellow DM&IR colors with the new reporting marks for the EJ&E.

Speaking of ore cars, DM&IR ore cars have often been part of the through all-rail ore trains operating to steel mills served by "The J," or for interchange from a western line to an eastern railroad. During the past 15 years or more, the Wisconsin Central often handled DM&IR ore cars in solid trains for delivery to the EJ&E. The DM&IR ore cars are mentioned partly because of the fact that the EJ&E was once a sister railroad of the DM&IR, as mentioned elsewhere in this book. As this is being written in mid-2004, the Canadian National Railway has purchased the DM&IR, and is now part of the CN System.

FLAT CARS. The EJ&E's flat car fleet was (and is) designed for service with and for the steel industry as well as a host of many other products. The cars ranged in length from the 40-foot lengths to over 88 feet. Part of the fleet was equipped with bulkheads for wall board service. Still other cars were designed for coiled steel service, both with and without covers. Part of the equipment was designed for handling steel bars, rails, and steel slab traffic. The flat car fleet was well designed for the variety of traffic originating on the EJ&E.

The EJ&E once owned and operated two tank cars. It was the smallest fleet of any group of cars on the railroad.

The following photos illustrate the interesting variety of the railroad's fleet of these various car types. ❏

Car 41330 (from the large 40000–41699 group) was an offset-side design with a 50-ton capacity and ribbed ends, painted black with white lettering including the full EJ&E insignia. There were some variables within this group of hoppers. For example, what appears to be car 40003 (the final digit is smudged) is within the number series but notice the rounded top of the car end, whereas the 41330 has a flat top. The cars were operated in a wide variety of coal service on the EJ&E, and are shown here at Joliet on October 19, 1952. *(Chet McCoid photo, Bob's Photo collection)*

Coal hopper 40369 was built in 1940 and by the time of this photograph at Minooka on August 12, 1973, had been uprated to 55 tons for its 2140 cubic feet capacity. Its rib-side design shows the diversity of the 40000–41699 group. On this repainted car, all lettering is Gothic.

(Bruce R. Meyer photo,
Alan Turner collection)

In the 100-ton hopper category, one example was triple hopper car 76014 from the 76000–76039 series. *(Frank Schnick)*

From early days, the EJ&E owned unusual side-dumping hopper cars. This one, built by Standard Steel Car Company in 1904, has loading lines at the left of the car side for, successively, ore, crushed stone, and granulated cinders. The large wheel at the left end of this view controlled unloading through the dump doors. In later years, a very similar design was used for coke service.

(Standard Steel Car Company photo, D. Keith Retterer collection)

The EJ&E coke car 73000 is an example of the high cubic capacity required for handling coke from the coke plant at U.S. Steel Gary Works for the steelmaking process. This operation is completely within the Gary Works complex and thus the coke cars are rarely seen outside the plant property.

(Elgin, Joliet and Eastern Railway)

This builder photo shows one of the big four-compartment Center Flow covered hoppers, cars 3000–3023, purchased by EJ&E in 1972, with 5250 cubic feet capacity and with a nominal capacity of 121 tons.   *(ACF Industries photo, Edward S. Kaminski collection)*

An example of a rebuilt covered hopper, converted for ballast service, is EJ&E car 113. The car was painted black with Gothic lettering and the "J" insignia. The equipment was in service at Kirk Yard in October 2003.   *(Patrick C. Dorin)*

Still other equipment operated for stone and ballast service are these examples of two types of cars with CRDX (Chicago Freight Car Leasing) reporting marks. The yellow cars were in service at Kirk Yard when photographed in October 2003. This is one more example of the diversity of equipment that can be operated for stone and ballast service.   *(both, Patrick C. Dorin)*

The EJ&E acquired a group of ore cars that had been converted to ballast service from the Duluth, Missabe & Iron Range Railway. The cars retained their yellow color scheme with a fresh coat over the DM&IR insignia and number, and the reporting marks EJ&E and the new car number added. A group of four are shown here at Kirk Yard in October, 2003. The cars have been modified from their configuration on the DM&IR, with repositioning of the air brake hose at the car ends. The DM&IR, for safety reasons, had placed the air brakes hoses above the couplers. That location meant that carmen and train crews no longer had to bend down between the cars, in close proximity of the car wheels, to couple the air hoses. Note how the wheels extend beyond the end of the car in this photo. *(Patrick C. Dorin)*

As a final sidebar note: When the author was on staff for the EJ&E, a study was made on the possibility of securing a fleet of ore cars for use in the movement of ore and stone. This did not happen then, but here we are in the 21st century, and ore cars, converted for ballast service, are now in service on the "J". *(Patrick C. Dorin)*

Although dump cars are neither revenue cars like hopper cars, nor are they strictly ballast cars, they do have unique unloading capabilities. The cars are often used in revenue stone service as well as work car service moving dirt or ballast. Car 37's portrait was taken at East Joliet in October 2003. The car was part of a block of cars operating in stone service. *(Patrick C. Dorin)*

FLAT CARS

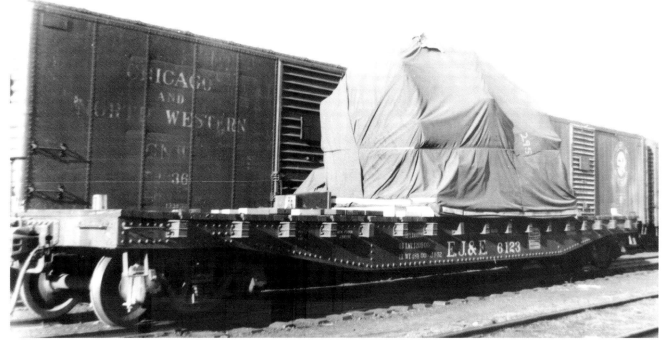

Prior to 1929 the largest flat cars owned by the EJ&E were 36-foot cars of 40 tons capacity. In that year the railroad took delivery of 75 new cars, 50-ton flat cars with fishbelly steel side and center sills, and 50 feet long overall, and soon joined by 65 more cars, bringing the series to 6000–6139. EJ&E 6123 was photographed in the early 1950s carrying some kind of machinery that was well protected with tarps. Note the Andrews trucks, something of an anachronism on cars built as late as1929. *(Ed Mines collection)*

Another 160 new flat cars in the 6215–6374 series joined the EJ&E roster in 1932. They were of the same design as the 1929 cars except for their trucks, which were an ARA cast steel design with spring planks and Barber lateral motion bolsters. EJ&E 6218 was carrying a pair of large sheet metal ducts when photographed in the early 1970s. *(Richard Hendrickson collection)*

The EJ&E found itself in need of additional flat cars to handle World War II traffic and prevailed upon the War Production Board to get two hundred new "war emergency" flat cars, 53 feet, 6 inches long, in the 6375–6574 series. At San Diego in the late 1960s, No. 6559 was painted green with orange lettering and was carrying new pressure cookers to a fish cannery.   *(Richard Hendrickson)*

In 1947 another 200 flat cars of the 6575–6774 series were placed in service which were essentially the same as the World War II cars except that they had steel floor stringers instead of wood. Here is EJ&E 6767 shortly after it was delivered in August of 1947 by American Car & Foundry. Trucks were Barber Stabilized S-2s.   *(Jay Williams collection)*

Car 6805 from the 6800–6827 series of 53-foot, 6-inch flat cars had been equipped with two large containers or hoods when photographed at Los Angeles in February 1961. The car is dark green with orange lettering, but the hoods are orange with black lettering. The reason for this arrangement isn't known.   *(Morris Abowitz photo, Bill Sheehan collection)*

These two photo illustrate both sides of a wood cupola caboose with two windows on each side and lettered with Roman lettering. Caboose 138 was at Joliet on October 18, 1952. One view shows it arriving on a freight train; in the other view it has been moved to the caboose track.

(both, Chet McCoid photos, Bob's Photo collection)

Chapter 12

CABOOSES AND WORK CARS

EJ&E cabooses can rank among some of the most interesting groups of cars to be found anywhere, especially with regional railroads. The railroad operated a variety of wood cabooses through to the 1960s, which included cars for over the road, transfer and special switching moves. Steel cars were also added to the fleet, and were among the best cars to be found. Most, if not all, of the fleet was painted in the full orange color scheme. There was a variety of lettering, including insignias and numbering systems.

The photos illustrate the vast diversity found with the EJ&E caboose fleet, of which a fair number are still in operation in 2004. There is no doubt about it, the caboose was the best way to end a freight train.

WORK CARS. The EJ&E owns and operates a variety of work cars for maintenance work. The following photos illustrate some of the different work cars in operation on the J. Most of the work cars were painted in the orange color scheme with black lettering. ❏

Wooden caboose 112 is a prime example of the cars without cupolas operated in transfer or switching service during the 1940s through into the 1960s. The cars were orange with Roman lettering and included the full EJ&E "Outer Belt" insignia. This car was photographed at Waukegan in June, 1965. *(Don Degner photo, J. Michael Gruber collection)*

Still another example of a wood caboose, in somewhat derelict condition, was the 8763 which was a new number. The car was photographed at Waukegan in June 1965.

(Don Degner photo, J. Michael Gruber collection)

Steel transfer caboose 197 was assigned to Gary in 1987 when its portrait was taken at Kirk Yard. The car made numerous trips within the yard as well as to the various steel making facilities in the area.

(Frank Schnick)

In this photo, transfer caboose 197 was assigned to a set of work cars which were at Griffith, Indiana during the spring of 2000.

(Patrick C. Dorin)

Steel road caboose 503 displays the latest of the lettering schemes as of 2000, which in this case were simply a Gothic EJ&E and the car number. Note the center window has been blocked out. Griffith, Indiana in April 2000.

(Patrick C. Dorin)

Caboose 504 illustrates the original letter and orange paint applications on the 500-series road cabooses. Note the Roman lettering and the full EJ&E insignia. The lettering was a silver/white color with a thin black outline. The 504 was between freight runs at Waukegan in October, 1966.

(Harold K. Vollrath collection)

This view shows the other side of caboose 504, repainted without the full EJ&E insignia but with Roman lettering and numbers in green, shown at Kirk Yard, 1987.

(Patrick C. Dorin)

Caboose 505 in the simplified orange scheme with green lettering.

(Frank Schnick)

Caboose 506 had a different assignment. It is 1987 and the car is painted in a full orange scheme with Gothic lettering to the left. Below the cupola is lettered "M of E" (Maintenance of Equipment) with the words "Diner Car" below. The small "J" insignia is below the center window. The car was assigned to Kirk Yard.

(Patrick C. Dorin)

These two cabooses, cars 509 and 532, are being switched for a freight train run at East Joliet Yard. Note the marker lights on No. 509. The 532 was being deadheaded to balance the caboose supply. *(Russ Porter)*

Caboose 520 also had an "M of E" assignment like car 506 but as a sleeper car. Note the electric cable connecting No. 520 and the 506 at the right of the photo. *(Frank Schnick)*

Faded caboose 533 was photographed at Kirk Yard in October 2003. As was the case for many of the cars, the center window has been blocked off.

(Patrick C. Dorin)

Caboose 539 in the original colors with the full EJ&E insignia lays over between freight runs at Waukegan. The car was assigned to train operations out of East Joliet Yard.

(Russ Porter)

Caboose 540 in the original scheme, spotted behind the roundhouse at Kirk Yard in the 1970s.

(Patrick C. Dorin)

In the mid-1980s, car 540 carried the Gothic paint scheme without insignias, as shown in this 1987 portrait at Kirk Yard.

(Frank Schnick)

In 2003, almost 30 years later, caboose 540 has had some paint scheme changes. The lettering and numbers are barely visible on the badly faded orange at Kirk Yard.

(Patrick C. Dorin)

This view shows caboose 546 with green Roman Lettering.

(Patrick C. Dorin)

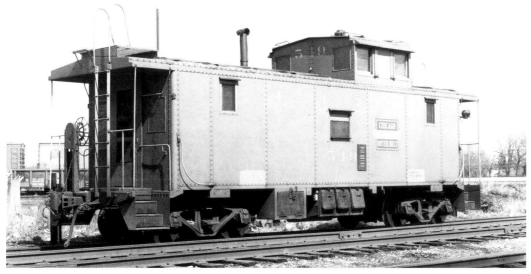

For a final shot, let's take a look at car 549 as it once looked with the full EJ&E insignia. The car was at La Porte, Indiana in March 1973.

(Ted Schnepf collection)

Flat car 8737 originally operated in revenue service, but was eventually converted to "Company Service Only" with extended sides. It was seen at Joliet on October 19, 1952. *(Chet McCoid photo, Bob's Photo collection)*

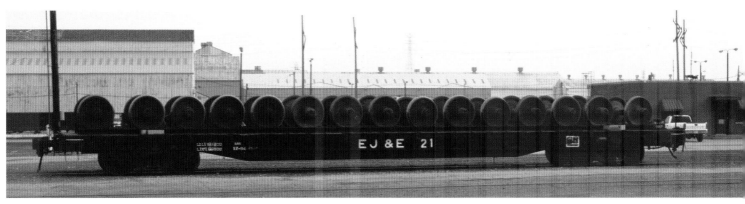

Flat car 21 was assigned to "Wheel Car" service when its portrait was taken at Kirk Yard in October 2003. *(Patrick C. Dorin)*

Flat car 8148 was painted black with Gothic lettering and red end panels at both ends of the car when photographed at Kirk Yard in October 2003. *(Patrick C. Dorin)*

Bunk Car 8731 was stored at Griffith, Indiana when photographed in August 2000. It is recognizably a former World War II troop sleeper, converted to other use. The car was typical of many EJ&E work cars and cabooses and was painted in the full orange color scheme.

(Patrick C. Dorin)

EJ&E converted a number of former heavyweight passenger cars for various types of work car service, including bunk cars, food service cars, and tool storage. This string was at East Joliet in 1972.

(Russ Porter)

Here is an example of the combination car converted for work car service coupled to the car in the previous photo at East Joliet.

(Russ Porter)

Appendix 1

FREIGHT EQUIPMENT ROSTERS

The following set of rosters from the 1950s through to the early part of the 21st century (2003) lists the revenue freight equipment in service on the EJ&E for more than 50 years. These listings are from EJ&E records and from *Official Railway Equipment Registers*. In Tables 2–5, coiled steel cars are listed with flat cars or gondolas.

Table 1
E&JE FREIGHT EQUIPMENT, 1950s

Group & Number Series	Inside Length	Remarks	Group & Number Series	Inside Length	Inside Height, Remarks
Box Cars			**Gondolas**		
7300–7799	40' 6"	6-foot single door	32750–33249	49'	3', drop ends
60400–61399	40' 6"	8-foot single door	33250–34189	48' 6"	3', drop ends
			34200–34899	49' 1"	3', drop ends
Covered Hoppers			34900–35399	48' 6"	3', drop ends
3000–3049	26' 4"	70-ton capacity	80000–80499	46' 3"	4'
3050–3199	29' 3"	70-ton	80500–80999	48' 6"	3'
			90000–90099	65'	3' 6"
Open Hoppers			90100–90299	65' 6"	3' 6"
600–644	28'	flue dust service			
40000–41699	34' 9"	50-ton twin	**Tank Cars**		
41700–41999	34' 9"	50-ton	16, 17		
70000–70899	39' 7"	70-ton, coke service			
70900–71249	39' 7"	70-ton, ballast service	**Flat Cars**		
			700–945	32' 8"	
Gondolas	**Inside Length**	**Inside Height, Remarks**	5000–5199	48' 6"	
			6000–6374	50'	
400–407	40'	4'	6375–6774	53' 6"	14 with bulkheads, IL 45' 10" or 48' 6"
25197, 25593	34' 3"	3' 8", AAR designation GD	8000–8299	36'	
30600–30899	40'	4'			
31000–31549	49'	3'	**Air Dump Cars**		
31550–32449	49'	3'	200–249, 300–319		
32450–32749	48' 6"	3', drop ends			

Table 2
EJ&E FREIGHT EQUIPMENT, 1960s

Group & Number Series	Inside Length	Remarks	Group & Number Series	Inside Length	Inside Height, Remarks
Box Cars			**Gondolas**		
60000–60199	38' 4"	8' single door, tin plate service	4500–4584	49'	3', covered for coil steel service
60300–60324	40' 6"	8' single door	4700–4709	49'	4' 7", covered, with bulkheads for sheet steel loading
60400–61399	40' 6"	8' single door			
62000–62074	50' 4"	10' single door	30600–30899	40'	4'
62999	50' 7"	14' double door	31000–32449	49'	3'
63000–63074	50' 6"	10' single door, cushion underframe	32450–32749	48' 6"	3', slab loading, orange side panels at each end
64000–64299	40' 6"	7' 8" single door	32750–33249	49'	3'
65000–65179	50' 6"	14' double door	33250–34189	48' 6"	3'
			34200–34899	49' 1"	3'
Covered Hoppers			34900–35399	48' 6"	3'
3100–3199	29' 3"	70-ton, 1958 cubic feet	80000–80014	52' 6"	3', equipped with channel upright stakes for diagonal plate loading
3200–3405	29' 3"	70-ton, 2003 cubic feet			
3500–3515	54' 6"	100-ton, 4740 cubic feet	80500–80999	48' 6"	3' 2"
3525–3546	54' 6"	100-ton, 4740 cubic feet	81000–81599	42'	3' 10"
			82000–82399	52' 6"	4'
3600–3602	29' 3"	70-ton, 2003 cubic feet	90000–90099	65'	3' 6"
3700–3712	29' 3"	70-ton, 2003 cubic feet	90100–90499	65' 6"	3' 6"
			90500–90549	66'	5' 6"
3800–3809	29' 3"	70-ton, 2003 cubic feet			
3900–3911	29' 3"	70-ton, 2003 cubic feet	**Tank Cars**		
			16, 17		
Open Hoppers					
40000–41699	34' 9"	50-ton	**Flat Cars**		
41700–41999	34' 9"	50-ton	5000–5099	48' 6"	5000–5084 equipped with bulkheads for wall board loading
70000–70899	39' 7"	70-ton, coke service			
70900–71249	39' 7"	50-ton	6000–6374	50'	
72000–72198	40' 8"	70-ton	6375–6774	53' 6"	
			6800–6827	53' 6"	
Gondolas	**Inside Length**	**Inside Height, Remarks**	6850–6884	53' 6"	
			6899	49' 6"	
1000–1069	49'	3', coil steel service	6900–6919	53' 6"	equipped for coil steel loading
4000–4050	48' 6"	3', coil steel service, green panel at each end	7000–7050	48'	removable covers for coil steel service
			10000, 10001	53' 6"	equipped with load restraining chains

Table 3
EJ&E FREIGHT EQUIPMENT, 1980s

Group & Number Series	Inside Length	Remarks	Group & Number Series	Inside Length	Inside Height, Remarks
Box Cars			**Gondolas**		
62000–62074	50' 4"	10' single door	3800	52' 6"	3' 10", covered for coil steel service
62999	50' 7"	14' double door			
63000–63074	50' 6"	10' single door, cushion underframe	3900–3931	52' 6"	3' 10", covered, cushion underframe
63100–63174	50' 6"	14' double door	3932	52' 6"	3' 6", covered
63200	50' 6"	14' double door	3933–3936, 3941	52' 6",	3' 6", covered, cushion underframe
63201	50' 6"	cushion underframe			
62202	50' 6"	10' single door	3937–3940	52' 6"	3' 6"
63400–63409	50' 6"	14' double door	4006–4112	48' 6"	3', coil steel service, cushion underframe
63500–63584	50' 6"	14' double door			
65000–65274	50' 6"	14' double door			
65275–65279	50' 6"	10' single door	4200–4349	52' 6"	4', coil steel service, white panel at each end
65290–65296	50' 6"	10' single door			
65300–65334	50' 6"	10' single door	4350–4409	52' 6"	4', coil steel service, white panel at each end, Car 4402 equipped with bulkheads
Covered Hoppers					
3000–3023	53' 7"	Center Flow cars, 5250 cubic feet			
3200–3399	29' 3"	77-ton, 2003 cubic feet	4410–4549	52' 6"	4', coil steel service, white panel at each end
3500–3515	54' 6"	100-ton, 4740 cubic feet			
3525–3546	54' 6"	100-ton, 4740 cubic feet	4600–4632	52' 6"	3' 10", cushion underframe, covers, bulkheads
Open Hoppers			4635–4664	51' 11"	4', cushion underframe, roof, bulkheads
50–79	29' 3"	77-ton			
71000–71163	41' 8"	77-ton			
73000–73300	58' 9"	73-ton, coke service	4700–4799	52' 6"	4' 6", coil steel service
74000–74495	40' 7"	77-ton	4800–4849	52' 6"	4', coil steel service
76000–76039	48' 2"	100-ton	4965–4999	52' 6"	4' 6", coil steel service
Gondolas	**Inside Length**	**Inside Height, Remarks**	34900–35427	49'	3' 2"
1000–1069	49'	3'	80000–80014	52' 6"	3', drop ends, stakes for diagonal plate loading
2000–2049	52' 6"	4', bar steel service			
2050–2099	52' 6"	4', coil steel service, white panel at each end	82000–82399	52' 6"	4'
			83000–84399	52' 11"	3' 9"
			84400–85011	52' 11"	3' 9"
			86000–86126	50' 11"	4' 2"
			87000–88149	52' 6"	4'

Group & Number Series	Inside Length	Inside Height, Remarks	Group & Number Series	Inside Length	Inside Height, Remarks
Gondolas			**Flat Cars**		
88500–88899	52' 6"	4' 6"	5400–5409	49' 7"	coiled bar service
90100–90299	65' 6"	3' 6", drop ends	5600–5619	53' 6"	coiled bar service
90300–90499	66'	3' 6"	6300	53'	
90600–90699	66'	5' 6"	6301–6336	53' 6"	
90700–90899	66'	5' 6"	6375–6774	53' 6"	
90900–90946	65' 6"	3' 6", drop ends	6800–6829	53' 6"	covers, coiled steel service
91000–91199	65' 6"	3' 6"	6830–6949	53' 6"	covers, coiled steel service
Flat Cars			6950–7238	48'	covers, coiled steel service
5000–5074	48' 6"	bulkheads for wallboard service	8000–8146	53' 6"	
5085–5126	48' 6"	bulkheads	8500, 8501	82' 6"	moveable bulkheads, restricted loading
5200–5214	50' 7"	bulkheads, equipped with tie-downs	10000, 10001	56' 8"	bulkheads
5215–5229	48' 2"	bulkheads	601111	29' 4"	100-ton
5300	49' 6"	bulkheads			
5301	48' 2"				

Table 4
EJ&E FREIGHT EQUIPMENT, 1990s

Group & Number Series	Inside Length	Remarks	Group & Number Series	Inside Length	Inside Height, Remarks
Box Cars			**Gondolas**		
62000–62074	50' 4"	10' single door	4635–4664	51' 11"	4', cushion underframe, roof, bulkheads
63000–63074	50' 6"	10' single door, cushion underframe			
65275–65279	50' 6"	10' single door	4800–4874	52' 6"	4', coil steel service
65290–65296	50' 6"	10' single door			
65300–65334	50' 6"	10' single door	Cars 6800–7359 are equipped with covers for coil steel service.		
Covered Hoppers			6800–6830	48'	3' 9"
3000–3023	53' 7"	Center Flow cars, 5250 cubic feet	6850–6949	48'	3' 10"
			6950–7049	48'	3' 11"
3200–3399	29' 3"	77-ton, 2003 cubic feet	7050–7099	48'	3' 9"
			7100–7238	48'	3' 10"
3500–3515	54' 6"	100-ton, 4740 cubic feet	7300–7359	53' 4"	7' 5"
			18500–18999	52' 6"	4'
3525–3546	54' 6"	100-ton, 4740 cubic feet	80000–80014	52' 6"	3', drop ends, stakes for diagonal plate loading
Open Hoppers	**Outside Length**		80019	52' 6"	4'
			82004–82399	52' 6"	4'
42200–42283	43' 2"	77-ton	83003–84399	52' 11"	3' 9"
44000–44099	42' 8"	77-ton	84400–85011	52' 11"	3' 9"
71000–71163	45' 4"	77-ton	86000–86126	50' 11"	4' 2"
73000–73300	62' 11"	70-ton, coke service	87000–88143	52' 6"	4'
75000–75139	44' 4"	77-ton	88300–88399	52' 6"	5'
			88500–88899	52' 6"	4' 6"
Gondolas	**Inside Length**	**Inside Height, Remarks**	89501–89540	52' 6"	4' 6"
3800–3891	52' 6"	3' 10", covers, cushion underframe, coil steel service	90207–90299	65' 6"	3' 6", drop ends
			90300–90499	66'	3' 6"
3900–3909	52' 6"	3' 10", cushion underframe	90600–90699	66'	5' 6"
			90700–90899	66'	5' 6"
3910–3919	51' 11"	4', cushion underframe	91000–91198	65' 6"	3' 6"
4000–4199	48' 6"	3', coil steel service	**Flat Cars**		
4200–4348	52' 6"	4', coil steel service, white panels at each end	700–701	41' 8"	slab loading
			750–887	45'	slab loading
			896–998	45'	slab loading
4350–4409	52' 6"	4', coil steel service, white panel at each end	6000–6119	60'	
			6200–6299	60'	
			6300	53'	
4410–4549	52' 6"	4', coil steel service, white panel at each end	6301–6336	53' 6"	
			6375–6774	53' 6"	
			8000–8146	53' 6"	
			8500–8511	82' 6"	moveable bulkheads, restricted loading

Table 5
EJ&E FREIGHT EQUIPMENT—THE 21st CENTURY

Group & Number Series	Outside Length	Remarks
Box Cars		
65290–65291	55' 4"	10' single door
65294–65296	54' 11"	10' single door
Covered Hoppers		
None		
Open Hoppers		
108–118	35' 3"	100-ton
1000–1134	49' 9"	coke service

Gondolas	Outside Length	Height above rail, Remarks
40–46	57' 10"	9" 4"
3800–3891	60'	14' 6", cushion underframe, cover, coil steel service
3910–3924	57' 10"	9' 4", cushion underframe

All cars numbered 4000–7699 are equipped for coil steel service.

4000–4025	56' 7"	7' 7"
4065–4199	56' 7"	7' 7"
4200–4348	55' 11"	7' 7"
4350–4409	56' 5"	7' 7"
4410–4549	56' 7"	7' 7"
4641–4654	57' 10"	9' 4", covered
4700–4759	60' 4"	6' 2"
4800–4874	56' 7"	7' 7"
6800–6830	57' 8"	13' 4", covered
6850–6949	57' 8"	13' 10", covered

Group & Number Series	Outside Length	Height above rail, Remarks
Gondolas		
All cars 6950–699 are covered for coil steel service		
6950–6999	57' 8"	13' 4"
7000–7049	57' 8"	13' 4"
7050–7099	57' 6"	13' 4"
7100–7238	57' 8"	13' 4"
7300–7359	60' 4"	13' 4"
7400–7499	57' 11"	13' 6"
7500–7699	52' 2"	9' 2"
18500–18999	58' 5"	7' 7"
87000–88143	56' 7"	7' 7", varied numbers within group
87568	56' 7"	14'
87713, 88036	56' 7"	14'
87777	57' 2"	8' 9"
88300–88399	57' 2"	8' 9"
88500–88899	57' 1"	8' 1"
89100–89217	57' 7"	8' 2"
90800–90899	70' 7"	9' 2"
92000–92007	70' 7"	13' 10"
Flat Cars		
6000–6119	64' 10"	
6200–6249	65'	
6401	56' 9"	cushion underframe
6402–6453	56' 9"	
8500–8511	88' 5"	

Freight Schedules for Various Years

1945

COAL CITY BRANCH
BETWEEN WALKER AND COAL CITY
JOLIET DIVISION—WESTERN SUBDIVISION

EASTWARD		TIME TABLE No. 8 JANUARY 1, 1945 STATIONS	WESTWARD		
Telegraph and Telephone Stations	Distance From East Joliet		Station Numbers	Capacity of Station Tracks	Railroad Connections
DN TO P	9.90	Leave ....WALKER.... Arrive	15	122	....
		4.11			
....	14.01	...CATON FARM...	16	28	....
		7.44			
P	21.45	.....MINOOKA....	17	27	CRI&P
		6.19			
P	27.64	......DIVINE.....	18	43	....
		1.82			
P	29.46	.....CLAY PIT....	18A	61	....
		1.75			
....	31.21	...DELL ABBEY...	19		....
		4.03			
....	35.24	...COAL CITY.... Arrive Leave	21		....

Service has been discontinued on the Coal City Branch between Dell Abbey and Coal City.

Freight service is maintained between Walker and Dell Abbey daily except Sunday.

AURORA BRANCH
BETWEEN AURORA AND NORMANTOWN
JOLIET DIVISION—WESTERN SUBDIVISION

EASTWARD		THIRD CLASS 32 Freight Daily Ex. Sun.	TIME TABLE No. 8 JANUARY 1, 1945 STATIONS	SECOND CLASS 31 Freight Daily Ex. Sun.	WESTWARD	
Telegraph and Telephone Stations	Distance From Aurora				Station Numbers	Capacity of Station Tracks
		AM	Leave Arrive	AM		
P	......	9 40	......AURORA......	9 00	25	45
	1.00	9 50	...AURORA JCT.....	8 40	25	Wye
	1.81	9 55	...EAST AURORA*...	8 35	25	50
	6.40	10 10	......WOLFS.......	8 20	26	15
Des TO P	9.55	10 20	...NORMANTOWN... Arrive Leave	8 10	14	42
		AM		AM		

Trains starting from Aurora will obtain their orders and/or clearance Form A on telephone from operator at Eola.

*Interchange with C. M. St. P. & P.

JOLIET BRANCH
BETWEEN EAST JOLIET AND JOLIET
JOLIET DIVISION—WESTERN SUBDIVISION

EASTWARD		TIME TABLE No. 8 JANUARY 1, 1945 STATIONS	WESTWARD	
Telegraph and Telephone Stations	Coal and Water		Station Numbers	Capacity of Station Tracks
DN TO P	CW	Leave .....EAST JOLIET...... Arrive	30	Yard
DN TO P	....	2.36 ....JOLIET........ Arrive Leave	30	71

ROCKDALE BRANCH
BETWEEN ROCKDALE JCT. AND ROCKDALE
JOLIET DIVISION—WESTERN SUBDIVISION

EASTWARD		TIME TABLE No. 8 JANUARY 1, 1945 STATIONS	WESTWARD	
Telegraph and Telephone Stations	Distance From East Joliet		Station Numbers	Capacity of Station Tracks
P	3.46	Leave ....ROCKDALE JCT......... Arrive	29	....
		3.20		
....	6.66	...........DUBLIN............	72	13
		3.26		
P	9.92	.........ROCKDALE......... Arrive Leave	71	194

BETWEEN CAVANAUGH AND GARY
GARY DIVISION

Telegraph and Telephone Stations	EASTWARD		TIME TABLE No. 8	WESTWARD		Distance From East Joliet
	SECOND CLASS			SECOND CLASS		
	44 Freight	42 Freight	JAN. 1, 1945	43 Freight	41 Freight	
	Daily	Daily	STATIONS	Daily	Daily	
	PM	AM	Leave Arrive	AM	PM	
P	11 30	10 35	.CAVANAUGH.	8 20	9 20	42.86
			3.67			
DNTOP	11 55	11 00	.....GARY.....	8 05	9 00	46.53
			(Kirk Yard)			
	PM	AM	Arrive Leave	AM	PM	
	44	42		43	41	
	Daily	Daily		Daily	Daily	

BETWEEN SOUTH CHICAGO AND GARY
GARY DIVISION

Telegraph and Telephone Stations	Coal and Water	Distance From South Chicago	TIME TABLE No. 8 JANUARY 1, 1945 STATIONS	Station Numbers	Capacity of Station Tracks
			EASTWARD WESTWARD		
			Leave Arrive		
P	W	....	.SOUTH CHICAGO.	101	Yard
			4.51		
P	....	4.51	.....WHITING.....	....	Yard
			2.15		
P	....	6.66	.INDIANA HARBOR.	....	Yard
			3.00		
P	....	9.66	...BUFFINGTON...	115	Yard
			2.71		
DN TO P	CW	12.37	.......GARY.......	143	Yard
			(Kirk Yard)		
			Arrive Leave		

RAILROAD CONNECTIONS—GARY DIVISION

South Chicago
- Chicago Short Line R'y.
- C. R. I. & P. R'y.
- I. C. R. R.
- B. & O. R. R.
- N. Y. C. R. R.
- Belt R'y of Chicago.

Whiting, B. & O. C. T. R. R.

Indiana Harbor, I. H. B. R. R.

Pine, N. Y. C. R. R.

Curtis, B. & O. R. R.

Clark
- Wabash R. R.
- Penna. R. R.

Goff, C. S. S. & S. B. R'y.

GENERAL INSTRUCTIONS
GARY—DIVISION

1. The Gary Division between South Chicago and Gary and between Cavanaugh and Gary is double track and yard limits over which trains and engines may move without train orders, clearance card or time-table schedule.

The terminal of these main tracks at South Chicago is South Gate; at Gary, Kirk Yard Jct.; at Cavanaugh, No. 1 crossover.

Movements against the current of traffic must be authorized by yardmaster or conductor and protected as prescribed by Rule D-152 of the Operating Department.

Instructions to move against the current of traffic without protecting against opposing trains and engines must be in writing over the signature of the superintendent, or general yardmaster.

From sunset to sunrise, or when weather conditions require, trains and transfers with caboose on rear of train must display markers as prescribed by Rule 19, of the Operating Department, and transfers without caboose on rear must comply with Rule 19 (a), of the Operating Department.

Conductors of out-going trains and transfers must see that markers are not placed in brackets until train is ready to proceed, and on arrival at destination they must see that markers are removed as soon as train has stopped in clear on designated track.

Inbound trains and transfers must approach Kirk Yard Jct. prepared to stop, and will be governed by hand signal from switch tender. This signal will be given with a yellow flag by day and a yellow light by night. Unless otherwise instructed, crews on inbound trains will use the track assigned them by the switch tender.

2. Information regarding block signals 1177, 1169 and 1170, see Rule B-7 Joliet Division, Eastern Subdivision.

Trains must not exceed a speed of 35 miles per hour when approaching and passing bock signal 1177.

3. The station limits at Cavanaugh include No. 1 and No. 2 crossovers and the wye switch on 98th Street Branch.

4. REGISTER STATIONS: All trains to or from the Joliet Division will register at Gary (Kirk Yard).

BULLETIN ORDER BOARDS: South Chicago; Roundhouse, General Yardmaster's office, Yardmen's terminal building at 86th St. and at substation at east side of yard.

Gary (Kirk Yard); Roundhouse, General Yardmaster's office, substation in yard L, Yardmen's terminal building and East Gate.

Gary Mill Yard; Roundhouse, General Yardmaster's office, and Yardmen's terminal building.

STANDARD CLOCKS: South Chicago; Yardmen's terminal building at 86th Street.

Gary; Superintendent's office and General Yardmaster's office at Kirk Yard.

1945

JOLIET DIVISION—WESTERN SUBDIVISION—WAUKEGAN TO EAST JOLIET

Telegraph and Telephone Stations	Coal and Water	Capacity of Station Tracks	Capacity of Sidings	Distance From Waukegan	TIME TABLE No. 8 JANUARY 1, 1945 STATIONS	EASTWARD						
						SECOND CLASS					THIRD CLASS	
						4 Freight	8 Freight	6 Freight	10 Freight	12 Freight	32 Freight	18 Loc. Frt.
						Daily	Daily	Daily	Daily	Daily	Daily Ex. Sun.	Daily Ex. Sun.
						AM	AM	AM	PM	PM	AM	AM
DN TO P	CW	Yard	....	....	Leave ....WAUKEGAN....	4 30	....	8 45	2 30	8 45	....	6 45
					3.60							
P	....	53	42	3.60	.NORTH CHICAGO.	4 45	....	9 00	2 45	9 00	....	6 55
					2.39							
DN TO P	....	....	....	5.99	......UPTON.......	4 50	....	9 05	2 50	9 05	....	7 00
					1.52							
DN TO P	W	106	Westward 220	7.51	.....RONDOUT.....	5 00	....	9 15	3 00	9 15	....	7 20
					5.30							
DN TO P	....	74	85	12.81	....LEITHTON.....	5 20	....	9 35	3 20	9 35	....	7 45 [3]
					3.42							
....	....	23	....	16.23	....GILMER......	....						7 55
					3.63							
D TO P	W	53	77	19.86	..LAKE ZURICH...	5 45	....	10 00	3 45 [5]	10 00	....	8 25
					3.91							
DN TO P	....	86	91	23.77	...BARRINGTON...	5 55	....	10 10	3 55	10 10	....	8 45
					5.47							
P	....	12	79	29.25	.....SUTTON......	6 10	....	10 25 [17]	4 10	10 25	....	9 00
					6.20							
DN TO P	....	250	Westward 142	35.45	....SPAULDING....	6 30 [3]	9 00	10 45	4 30	10 45	....	9 20
					2.18							
....	....	55	....	37.63	....MUNGER......							
					1.90							
P	....	....	....	39.53	......WAYNE......	6 40	9 10	10 55	4 40	10 55	....	9 30
					2.77							
P	CW	....	....	42.30	....INGALTON.....	6 55	9 20	11 10	4 55	11 10	....	9 45
					1.49							
DN TO P	....	113	....	43.79	..WEST CHICAGO..	7 00	9 30	11 15	5 00	11 15	....	10 15
					4.32							
P	....	25	75	48.11	..WARRENHURST..	7 10	9 40	11 25	5 10	11 25	....	10 30
					2.20							
....	....	....	....	50.31	.ELECTRIC JCT...	....						
					.58							
DN TO P	....	118	73	50.89	......EOLA.......	7 25 [7]	9 50	11 35	5 20	11 35	....	10 50
					1.56							
P	....	....	72	52.45	...EAST SIDING...	7 30	9 55	11 40	5 25	11 40	....	10 55
					1.71							
P	....	17	124	54.16	....FRONTENAC....	7 35	10 00	11 45	5 30 [9]	11 45	....	11 10
					5.99							
Des TO P	....	42	Westward 94	60.15	..NORMANTOWN..	7 50 [17]	10 15	11 59	5 45	11 59	10 20	11 30
					3.03							
DN TO P	W	122	Westward 80	63.18	.....WALKER......	7 55 [31]	10 20	12 05	5 50	12 05	10 30	11 40
					.48							
Des	....	33	....	63.66	...PLAINFIELD....							
					.74							
P	....	119	....	64.40	...GRAVEL PIT....							
					1.05							
....	....	....	....	65.45	....ROGERS......							
					1.61							
P	....	....	....	67.06	.....COYNES......	8 05	10 30	12 15	6 00	12 15	10 45	11 50
					2.56							
P	....	....	....	69.62	.ROCKDALE JCT...							
					1.09							
P	....	77	....	70.71	...BRIDGE JCT....	8 15	10 40	12 25	6 10	12 25	10 55	12 05
					2.37							
DN TO P	CW	Yard	....	73.08	...EAST JOLIET... Arrive	8 30	11 00	12 45	6 30	12 45	11 15	12 25
						AM	AM	PM	PM	AM	AM	PM
						4	8	6	10	12	32	18
						Daily	Daily	Daily	Daily	Daily	Daily Ex. Sun.	Daily Ex. Sun.

JOLIET DIVISION—WESTERN SUBDIVISION—EAST JOLIET TO WAUKEGAN

Railroad Connections	Telegraph and Telephone Stations	Station Numbers	Distance From East Joliet	TIME TABLE No. 8 JANUARY 1, 1945 STATIONS	WESTWARD						
					SECOND CLASS						THIRD CLASS
					3 Freight Daily	7 Freight Daily	31 Freight Daily Ex. Sun.	5 Freight Daily	9 Freight Daily	11 Freight Daily	17 Loc. Frt. Daily Ex. Sun.
					AM	AM	AM	PM	PM	AM	PM
C&NW........	DN TO P	1	73.08	Arrive ....WAUKEGAN....	8 30	....	....	5 00	8 35	1 30	1 00
....	P	1½	69.48	.NORTH CHICAGO.	8 15	....	....	4 40	8 20	1 10	12 40
				3.60							
	DN TO P	1A	67.09	......UPTON.......	8 10	....	....	4 35	8 15	1 05	12 35
CMStP&P- CNS&M...... }	DN TO P	2	65.57	1.52 ....RONDOUT.....	8 05	....	....	4 30	8 10	1 00	12 30
				5.30							
Soo Line......	DN TO P	3	60.27	....LEITHTON.....	7 45 18	....	....	4 10	7 45	12 25	11 55
				3.42							
....		4	56.85	.....GILMER......	....	....	....	....	....	....	11 30
				3.63							
	D TO P	5	53.22	..LAKE ZURICH...	7 15	....	....	3 45 10	7 30	12 05	11 20
C&NW........	DN TO P	6	49.31	3.91 ...BARRINGTON...	7 05	....	....	3 30	7 20	11 55	10 55
				5.47							
....	P	7	43.83	......SUTTON......	6 45	....	....	3 10	7 00	11 30	10 25 6
				6.20							
CMStP&P....	DN TO P	8	37.63	...SPAULDING....	6 30 4	8 45	....	2 55	6 45	11 15	10 00
IC.............		9	35.45	2.18 ....MUNGER.....	....	....	....	....	....	....	....
CA&E........	P	9A	33.55	1.90 ......WAYNE......	6 05	8 20	....	2 30	6 30	11 00	9 45
CGW........	P	10	30.78	2.77 ....INGALTON.....	5 55	8 15	....	2 20	6 20	10 50	9 25
C&NW........	DN TO P	11	29.29	1.49 ..WEST CHICAGO..	5 40	7 50	....	2 05	6 00	10 35	9 05
				4.32							
....	P	12	24.97	..WARRENHURST..	5 25	7 35	....	1 55	5 50	10 25	8 45
CA&E........		12A	22.77	2.20 .ELECTRIC JCT...	....	....	....	....	....	....	....
CB&Q........	DN TO P	13	22.19	.58 ......EOLA.......	5 15	7 25 4	....	1 45	5 40	10 15	8 30
CB&Q........	P	13	20.63	1.56 ...EAST SIDING...	5 10	7 15	....	1 40	5 35	10 10	8 10
....	P	13A	18.92	1.71 ...FRONTENAC....	5 05	7 10	....	1 35	5 30 10	10 05	8 05
				5.99							
....	Des TO P	14	12.93	..NORMANTOWN..	4 50	6 55	8 10	1 20	5 05	9 50	7 50 4
	DN TO P	15	9.90	3.03 .....WALKER......	4 35	6 40	7 55 4	1 05	4 50	9 35	7 35
....	Des	27	9.42	.48 ...PLAINFIELD....	....	....	....	....	....	....	....
....	P	27A	8.68	.74 ..GRAVEL PIT....	....	....	....	....	....	....	....
....		27B	7.63	1.05 .....ROGERS......	....	....	....	....	....	....	....
				1.61							
....	P	28	6.02	......COYNES......	4 25	6 30	7 35	12 55	4 40	9 25	7 25
....	P	29	3.46	2.56 .ROCKDALE JCT...	....	....	....	....	....	....	....
....	P	29A	2.37	1.09 ...BRIDGE JCT....	4 10	6 10	7 25	12 40	4 25	9 10	7 15
Alton-AT&SF- CRI&P-MC- CMStP&P }	DN TO P	30	....	2.37 ...EAST JOLIET... Leave	4 00	6 00	7 15	12 30	4 15	9 00	7 05
					AM	AM	AM	PM	PM	PM	AM
					3	7	31	5	9	11	17
					Daily	Daily	Daily Ex. Sun.	Daily	Daily	Daily	Daily Ex. Sun.

3

98TH STREET BRANCH—JOLIET DIVISION—EASTERN SUBDIVISION
BETWEEN GRIFFITH AND 98TH STREET

Telegraph and Telephone Stations	Coal and Water	EASTWARD SECOND CLASS			TIME TABLE No. 8	WESTWARD SECOND CLASS			Distance From East Joliet	Distance From 98th Street	Station Numbers	Capacity of Station Tracks
		44 Freight	**42** Freight	**46** Freight	JANUARY 1, 1945	**43** Freight	**45** Freight	**41** Freight				
		Daily	Daily	Daily	STATIONS	Daily	Daily	Daily				
		PM	AM	AM		AM	PM	PM				
DN TO P	......	11 15	10 20	6 15	Leave · · · Arrive .....GRIFFITH.....	8 35	7 50	9 35	36.20	19.36	37	Yard
					3.55							
DN P		....	....	....	.....VAN LOON.....	....	....	....	39.75	15.81	61	....
					2.00							
P		....	....	....	.....IVANHOE.....	....	....	....	41.75	13.81	62	....
					1.11							
P	......	11 30	10 35	6 35	....CAVANAUGH....	8 20	7 30	9 20	42.86	12.70	63	Wye
					2.02							
P	W	....	....	6 50	.....SHEARSON.....		7 20		44.88	10.68	65	Wye
					3.25							
P		....	....	....	.....HAMMOND.....	....	....	....	48.13	7.43	45	51
					.58							
ᴅ		....	....	....	...STATE LINE....	....	....	....	48.71	6.85	46	Yard
					(C&WI) 4.87							
		....	....	....	..SOUTH DEERING..	....	....	....	53.58	1.98	....	....
					(BRC) 1.98							
P		....	....	....	..98TH STREET...	....	....	....	55.56	....	50	Yard
					Arrive · · · Leave							
		PM	AM	AM		AM	PM	PM				
		44	**42**	**46**		**43**	**45**	**41**				
		Daily	Daily	Daily		Daily	Daily	Daily				

WHITING BRANCH
BETWEEN SHEARSON AND WHITING
JOLIET DIVISION—EASTERN SUBDIVISION

Telegraph and Telephone Stations	Station Numbers	Coal and Water	EAST-WARD SECOND CLASS **46** Freight	TIME TABLE No. 8	WEST-WARD SECOND CLASS **45** Freight	Capacity of Sidings
			Daily	JANUARY 1, 1945 STATIONS	Daily	
			AM		PM	
P	65	W	6 50	Leave · · · Arrive ...SHEARSON...	7 20	72
				3.56		
DN TO P	60	W	7 15	....WHITING....	7 00	......
			AM	Arrive · · · Leave	PM	
			46		**45**	
			Daily		Daily	

Trains and engines will be governed by Rule 93 and may move without train orders, clearance card or time table schedule between Cavanaugh and State Line and between Shearson and Whiting, except trains and engines entering this territory at Cavanaugh and trains leaving Whiting en route to Griffith or Gary (Kirk Yard) must be authorized by clearance Form A, properly filled out.

Before crossing the tracks of the C. S. S. & S. B. Railroad east of Shearson on the Whiting Branch, train and switching movements must come to a complete stop not less than 40 feet nor more than 500 feet from the crossing, and a member of the crew must proceed to the crossing and ascertain there is no car or train on or closely approaching the crossing, and that it is safe to proceed before moving over the crossing. (See Rule B-34).

The jurisdiction of the general yardmaster at Whiting (E. J. & E.) includes Cavanaugh, Shearson, Hammond, State Line, 98th Street and Whiting (E. J. & E.).

JOLIET DIVISION—EASTERN SUBDIVISION—EAST JOLIET TO PORTER

EASTWARD

Telegraph and Telephone Stations	Coal and Water	Capacity of Station Tracks	Capacity of Sidings	Distance From East Joliet	TIME TABLE No. 8 — JANUARY 1, 1945 — STATIONS	10 Freight Daily	46 Freight Daily	42 Freight Daily	4 Freight Daily	6 Freight Daily	44 Freight Daily	50 Loc. Frt. Daily Ex. Sun.
						AM	AM	AM	PM	PM	PM	AM
DN TO P	CW	Yard			Leave EAST JOLIET...	2 00	4 00	8 05	1 00	6 00	9 00	7 05
P		10		2.65	2.65 MARBLE FALLS..							
DN TO P		66	73	8.22	5.57 BRISBANE.....	2 20	4 20	8 25	1 20	6 20	9 20	7 30
Des TO P	W	101		14.04	5.82 FRANKFORT....	2 40	4 40	8 45	1 40	6 40	9 40	8 00
DN TO P		138	80	21.60	7.56 MATTESON....	2 55	4 55	9 00	1 55	6 55	9 55	8 30
DN TO P		Yard	62 Westward	24.90	3.30 CHICAGO HEIGHTS	3 05	5 05	9 10 50	2 05	7 05	10 05	8 40 / 9 20 42
TO P	CW	130	85	31.29	6.39 DYER.......	3 30	5 30	9 35	2 30	7 30	10 30	9 45
_..♦ TO P		Yard	Eastward 218	33.81	2.52 HARTSDALE....	3 40	5 40	9 45	2 40	7 40	10 40	10 00
DN TO P		Yard	Westward 235	36.20	2.39 GRIFFITH.....	4 15	6 15	10 20	3 15	8 15	11 15	10 45
DN TO P	W	149	West 72 East 76	45.71	9.51 HOBART......	4 35 / 5 05 9	....	....	4 05	9 05 5	....	11 15 / 11 45 11
DN TO		110	58	52.10	6.39 McCOOL......	5 35	....	....	4 35	9 35	....	12 10
DN TO	W	56		53.47	1.37 CROCKER.....	5 50			4 50	9 50		12 20
DN TO P	CW	Yard		56.70	3.23 PORTER...... Arrive	6 15			5 15	10 15		12 45
						AM	AM	AM	PM	PM	PM	PM
						10 Daily	46 Daily	42 Daily	4 Daily	6 Daily	44 Daily	50 Daily Ex. Sun.

The jurisdiction of the general yardmaster at Dyer includes Chicago Heights, Dyer, Hartsdale, Griffith and Hobart.

JOLIET DIVISION—EASTERN SUBDIVISION—PORTER TO EAST JOLIET

WESTWARD

Railroad Connections	Telegraph and Telephone Stations	Station Numbers	Distance From Porter	TIME TABLE No. 8 — JANUARY 1, 1945 — STATIONS	9 Freight Daily	43 Freight Daily	11 Freight Daily	45 Freight Daily	41 Freight Daily	5 Freight Daily	51 Loc. Frt. Daily Ex. Sun.
					AM	AM	PM	PM	PM	AM	PM
Alton-AT&SF- CRI&P-MC- CMStP&P	DN TO P	30	56.70	Arrive EAST JOLIET..	7 45	10 45	2 45	9 45	11 45	12 15	12 30
	P	30A	54.05	2.65 MARBLE FALLS.							
Wabash	DN TO P	31	48.48	5.57 BRISBANE.....	7 15	10 20	2 15	9 20	11 20	11 45	12 05
	Des TO P	32	42.66	5.82 FRANKFORT...	7 00	10 05	2 00	9 05	11 05	11 30	11 40
ICRR	DN TO P	33	35.10	7.56 MATTESON....	6 45	9 45	1 45	8 45	10 45	11 15	11 15
C&EI-CHTT	DN TO P	34	31.80	3.30 CHICAGO HEIGHTS	6 30	9 35	1 30	8 35	10 35	11 00	10 50
CI&L	DN TO P	35	25.41	6.39 DYER......	6 05	9 10	1 00	8 15	10 10	10 30	10 10
PRR-MC-NYC	DN TO P	36	22.89	2.52 HARTSDALE....	5 35	8 45	12 35	8 00	9 45	10 05	9 40
Erie-C&O-GT.	DN TO P	37	20.50	2.39 GRIFFITH.....	5 25	8 35	12 25	7 50	9 35	9 55	9 30
NKP-PRR	DN TO P	38	10.99	9.51 HOBART......	4 35 10	....	11 35 50	....	....	9 05 6	8 40
B&O	DN TO	39	4.60	6.39 McCOOL......	3 30	....	10 30	....	....	8 00	7 40
Wabash	DN TO	40	3.23	1.37 CROCKER.....	3 15	....	10 15	....	....	7 45	7 20
NYC-PM	DN TO P	41		3.23 PORTER...... Leave	3 00	....	10 00	....	....	7 30	7 00
					AM	AM	AM	PM	PM	PM	AM
					9 Daily	43 Daily	11 Daily	45 Daily	41 Daily	5 Daily	51 Daily Ex. Sun.

Engines may move with the current of traffic between Hartsdale and Griffith (either direction) without a clearance Form A but, must not move between Hartsdale and Dyer without proper authority.

1956

JOLIET DIVISION—WESTERN SUBDIVISION—WAUKEGAN TO EAST JOLIET

Train Order and Telephone Stations	Capacity of Station Tracks	Capacity of Sidings	Distance From Waukegan	TIME TABLE No. 11 — JULY 8, 1956 — STATIONS	EASTWARD — SECOND CLASS					THIRD CLASS
					4 Freight Daily	6 Freight Daily	10 Freight Daily	12 Freight Daily		18 Loc. Frt. Daily Ex. Sun.
					AM	AM	PM	PM		AM
DN TO P	Yard	......	......	Leave WAUKEGAN	3 30	9 45	1 00	8 15	....	6 45
				3.60						
P	53	42	3.60	NORTH CHICAGO	3 45	10 00	1 10	8 30	....	6 55
				2.39						
DN TO P	......		5.99	UPTON	3 50	10 05	1 15	8 35	....	7 00
				1.52						
DN TO P	106	Westward 220	7.51	RONDOUT	4 00	10 15	2 00	8 45	....	7 05 / 7 20 3
				5.30						
DN TO P	74	85	12.81	LEITHTON	4 15	10 30	2 15	9 00	....	7 40
				7.05						
D* TO P	53	77	19.86	LAKE ZURICH	4 35	10 50 17	2 35	9 20	....	8 05
				3.91						
DN TO P	86	91	23.77	BARRINGTON	4 45	11 00	2 45 5	9 30	....	8 30
				5.47						
P	12	79	29.25	SUTTON	5 00	11 15	3 00	9 45	....	8 45
				6.20						
DN TO P	250	Westward 142	35.45	SPAULDING	5 15	11 30	3 15	10 00	....	9 00
				2.18						
	55	....	37.63	MUNGER						
				1.90						
P	....		39.53	WAYNE	5 25	11 40	3 25	10 10	....	9 10
				2.77						
P	....		42.30	INGALTON	....	....	....	....		9 45
				1.49						
DN TO P	113	....	43.79	WEST CHICAGO	5 35	11 50	3 35	10 25	....	9 45
				6.52						
		....	50.31	ELECTRIC JCT	....	....	....	....	....	
				.58						
P	118	97	50.89	EOLA	5 50	12 05	3 50	10 40	....	10 10
				1.56						
P	....	72	52.45	EAST SIDING	5 55	12 10	3 55	10 45	....	10 15
				1.71						
P	17	124	54.16	FRONTENAC	6 00	12 15	4 00	10 50	....	10 25
				5.99						
P	42	Westward {	60.15	NORMANTOWN	6 10	12 25	4 10	11 00	....	10 40
				3.03						
DN TO P	9	320 {	63.18	WALKER	6 15	12 30	4 15	11 05	....	10 50
				.48						
Des P	33	....	63.66	PLAINFIELD	....	....	....	......		
				.74						
P	119	....	64.40	GRAVEL PIT	....	....	....	....		
				2.66						
P	....		67.06	COYNES	6 25	12 40	4 25	11 15	....	11 00
				2.56						
P	....		69.62	ROCKDALE JCT	....	....	....	....		
				1.09						
DN TO P	77	....	70.71	BRIDGE JCT	6 35	12 50	4 35	11 25	....	11 10
				2.37						
P	Yard	....	73.08	EAST JOLIET Arrive	7 00	1 15	5 00	11 45	....	11 30
					AM	PM	PM	PM		AM

*Closed on Saturdays, Sundays and Holidays.

4	6	10	12		18
Daily	Daily	Daily	Daily		Daily Ex. Sun.

JOLIET DIVISION—WESTERN SUBDIVISION—EAST JOLIET TO WAUKEGAN

Railroad Connections	Train Order and Telephone Stations	Station Numbers	Distance From East Joliet	TIME TABLE No. 11 JULY 8, 1956 STATIONS	WESTWARD SECOND CLASS 3 Freight Daily	5 Freight Daily	9 Freight Daily	11 Freight Daily			THIRD CLASS 17 Loc. Frt. Daily Ex. Sun.
					AM	PM	PM	AM			PM
C&NW	DN TO P	1	73.08	Arrive ....WAUKEGAN....	7 45	4 00	7 45	12 30			12 15
	P	1½	69.48	3.60 .NORTH CHICAGO.	7 20	3 40	7 25	12 10			11 50
	DN TO P	1A	67.09	2.39 ......UPTON.......	7 15	3 35	7 20	12 05			11 40
CMStP&P- CNS&M	DN TO P	2	65.57	1.52 ....RONDOUT.....	7 10 13	3 30	7 15	12 01			11 35
Soo Line	DN TO P	3	60.27	5.30 ...LEITHTON.....	6 40	3 10	6 55	11 40			11 10
	D* TO P	5	53.22	7.05 ..LAKE ZURICH...	6 25	2 55	6 40	11 25			10 50 6
C&NW	DN TO P	6	49.31	3.91 ...BARRINGTON...	6 15	2 45 10	6 30	11 15			10 25
	P	7	43.83	5.47 ......SUTTON......	6 00	2 30	6 15	11 00			10 00
CMStP&P	DN TO P	8	37.63	6.20 ...SPAULDING....	5 45	2 15	6 00	10 45			9 45
IC		9	35.45	2.18 ...MUNGER.....	....	....	....	....			....
CA&E	P	9A	33.55	1.90 .....WAYNE......	5 30	2 00	5 45	10 30			9 15
CGW	P	10	30.78	2.77 ...INGALTON.....							
C&NW	DN TO P	11	29.29	1.49 ..WEST CHICAGO..	5 20	1 50	5 35	10 20			9 00
CA&E		12A	22.77	6.52 ...ELECTRIC JCT...	....						....
CB&Q	P	13	22.19	.58 ....EOLA........	5 05	1 35	5 20	10 05			8 25
CB&Q	P	13	20.63	1.56 ...EAST SIDING...	5 00	1 30	5 15	10 00			8 10
	P	13A	18.92	1.71 ....FRONTENAC....	4 55	1 25	5 10	9 55			8 05
	P	14	12.93	5.99 ...NORMANTOWN..	4 40	1 10	4 55	9 40			7 50
	DN TO P	15	9.90	3.03 .....WALKER......	4 30	1 00	4 45	9 30			7 35
	Des P	27	9.42	.48 ...PLAINFIELD....	....						....
	P	27A	8.68	.74 ...GRAVEL PIT...							
	P	28	6.02	2.66 ......COYNES......	4 20	12 50	4 35	9 20			7 25
	P	29	3.46	2.56 .ROCKDALE JCT...	....						....
	DN TO P	29A	2.37	1.09 ...BRIDGE JCT....	4 10	12 40	4 25	9 10			7 15
GM&O- AT&SF- CRI&P-MC- CMStP&P	P	30	....	2.37 ...EAST JOLIET... Leave	4 00	12 30	4 15	9 00			7 05
					AM	PM	PM	PM			AM

*Closed on Saturdays, Sundays and Holidays.

3 Daily	5 Daily	9 Daily	11 Daily			17 Daily Ex. Sun.

KIRK YARD LINE—BETWEEN GRIFFITH AND KIRK YARD
JOLIET—GARY DIVISIONS

Train Order and Telephone Stations	Distance From East Joliet	EASTWARD SECOND CLASS 44 Freight	EASTWARD SECOND CLASS 42 Freight	TIME TABLE No. 11 JULY 8, 1956	WESTWARD SECOND CLASS 43 Freight	WESTWARD SECOND CLASS 41 Freight	Distance From Kirk Yard	Station Numbers	Capacity of Station Tracks
		Daily	Daily	STATIONS	Daily	Daily			
		PM	AM	Leave Arrive	AM	PM			
DN TO P	36.20	10 40	9 45	..............GRIFFITH..............	8 35	9 30	10.33	37	Yard
DN P	39.75	....	....	3.55 ....VAN LOON...........	....	....	6.78	61	80
DN P	41.75	....	....	2.00 ....IVANHOE............	....	....	4.78	62	6
P	42.86	10 55	10 00	1.11 ....CAVANAUGH...........	8 15	9 10	3.67	63	Wye
DN TO P	46.53	11 15	10 15	3.67 ....KIRK YARD...........	8 05	9 00	....	143	Yard
		PM	AM	Arrive Leave	AM	PM			
		44	42		43	41			
		Daily	Daily		Daily	Daily			

WHITING BRANCH
BETWEEN CAVANAUGH AND WHITING
GARY DIVISION

Distance From Whiting	Train Order and Telephone Stations	TIME TABLE No. 11	Station Numbers	Capacity of Sidings
EASTWARD			WESTWARD	
		STATIONS		
5.58	P	Leave Arrive ...CAVANAUGH...	63	Wye
3.56	P	2.02 ....SHEARSON....	65	72
....	D* TO P	3.56 .....WHITING..... Arrive Leave	60	Yard

*Closed on Saturdays, Sundays and Holidays.

LAKE FRONT LINE
BETWEEN SOUTH CHICAGO AND KIRK YARD
GARY DIVISION

Train Order and Telephone Stations	Distance From South Chicago	TIME TABLE No. 11	Station Numbers	Capacity of Station Tracks
EASTWARD			WESTWARD	
		STATIONS		
P	....	Leave Arrive .SOUTH CHICAGO.	101	Yard
P	4.51	4.51 .....WHITING.....	....	Yard
P	6.66	2.15 .INDIANA HARBOR.	....	Yard
P	9.66	3.00 ...BUFFINGTON...	115	Yard
DN TO P	12.37	2.71 ....KIRK YARD.... Arrive Leave	143	Yard

PORTER LINE—EAST JOLIET TO PORTER
JOLIET DIVISION—EASTERN SUBDIVISION

	Train Order and Telephone Stations	Capacity of Station Tracks	Capacity of Sidings	Distance From East Joliet	TIME TABLE No. 11 JULY 8, 1956 / STATIONS	EASTWARD					THIRD CLASS	
						SECOND CLASS						
						42 Freight Daily	4 Freight Daily	6 Freight Daily	44 Freight Daily		50 Loc. Frt. Daily Ex. Sun.	
						AM	AM	PM	PM		AM	
....	DN TO P	Yard	....	....	Leave ...EAST JOLIET...	8 05	11 00	6 00	9 00	....	7 05	....
....	P		....	2.65	2.65 ...MARBLE FALLS..	....	....	....	....		....	....
....	DN TO P	139	....	8.22	5.57 ....BRISBANE.....	8 25	11 20	6 20	9 20	....	7 30	....
....	P	98	....	14.04	5.82 ....FRANKFORT....	8 45	11 40	6 40	9 40	....	8 00	....
....	DN TO P	Yard	79	21.60	7.56 ....MATTESON....	9 00	11 55	6 55	9 55		8 30	....
....	DN TO P	Yard	62	24.90	3.30 CHICAGO HEIGHTS	9 10 50	12 05	7 05	10 05		8 40 / 9 20 42	....
....	DN TO P	130	85	31.29	6.39 ......DYER.......	9 25	12 20	7 20	10 20		9 45	....
....	DN TO P	Yard	Eastward 218	33.81	2.52 ...HARTSDALE....	9 35	12 30	7 30	10 30		10 00	....
....	DN TO P	Yard	Westward 235	36.20	2.39 .....GRIFFITH.....	9 45	12 40	7 40	10 40		10 45	....
....	DN TO P	149	West 72 East 76	45.71	9.51 ......HOBART......	....	1 30	8 30	....		11 15 / 11 45 11	....
....	DN TO P	110	58	52.10	6.39 .....McCOOL......	....	1 55	8 55	....		12 10	....
....	DN TO P	56	....	53.47	1.37 ....CROCKER....	....	2 10	9 10	....		12 20	....
....	DN TO P	Yard	....	56.70	3.23 .....PORTER...... Arrive	....	2 30	9 30	....		12 45	....
						AM	PM	PM	PM		PM	
						42 Daily	4 Daily	6 Daily	44 Daily		50 Daily Ex. Sun.	

PORTER LINE—PORTER TO EAST JOLIET
JOLIET DIVISION—EASTERN SUBDIVISION

Railroad Connections	Train Order and Telephone Stations	Station Numbers	Distance From Porter	TIME TABLE No. 11 JULY 8, 1956 / STATIONS	WESTWARD					THIRD CLASS	
					SECOND CLASS						
					9 Freight Daily	43 Freight Daily	11 Freight Daily	41 Freight Daily		51 Loc. Frt. Daily Ex. Sun.	
					AM	AM	PM	PM		PM	
GM&O- AT&SF- CRI&P-MC- CMStP&P	DN TO P	30	56.70	Arrive ...EAST JOLIET...	4 15	10 15	1 35	11 10	....	12 30	....
....	P	30A	54.05	2.65 ...MARBLE FALLS..	....	....	....	....		....	....
Wabash........	DN TO P	31	48.48	5.57 .....BRISBANE.....	3 50	9 50	1 10	10 45		12 05	....
....	P	32	42.66	5.82 ....FRANKFORT...	3 35	9 35	12 55	10 30		11 40	....
IC............	DN TO P	33	35.10	7.56 ....MATTESON....	3 15	9 20	12 40	10 15		11 15	....
C&EI-CHTT. CMStP&P	DN TO P	34	31.80	3.30 CHICAGO HEIGHTS	3 05	9 10	12 30	10 05		10 50	....
MONON......	DN TO P	35	25.41	6.39 ......DYER.......	2 50	8 55	12 15	9 50		10 10	....
PRR-MC-NYC	DN TO P	36	22.89	2.52 ....HARTSDALE....	2 40	8 45	12 05	9 40		9 40	....
Erie-C&O-GT.	DN TO P	37	20.50	2.39 .....GRIFFITH.....	2 30	8 35	11 55	9 30		9 30	....
NKP-PRR....	DN TO P	38	10.99	9.51 ......HOBART......	2 00	....	11 20 50	....		8 40	....
B&O..........	DN TO P	39	4.60	6.39 ......McCOOL......	1 20	....	10 20	....		7 40	....
Wabash.......	DN TO P	40	3.23	1.37 .....CROCKER....	1 10	....	10 10	....		7 20	....
NYC-C&O....	DN TO P	41	....	3.23 .....PORTER...... Leave	1 00	....	10 00	....		7 00	....
					AM	AM	AM	PM		AM	
					9 Daily	43 Daily	11 Daily	41 Daily		51 Daily Ex. Sun.	

1965

	EASTWARD				Distance From Waukegan	TIME TABLE No. 1	Distance From East Joliet			WESTWARD		
THIRD CLASS	SECOND CLASS					MAY 1, 1965		SECOND CLASS				THIRD CLASS
18 Loc. Frt.	**12** Freight	**10** Freight	**6** Freight	**4** Freight				**3** Freight	**5** Freight	**9** Freight	**11** Freight	**17** Loc. Frt.
Daily Ex. Sun.	Daily	Daily	Daily	Daily		STATIONS		Daily	Daily	Daily	Daily	Daily Ex. Sun.
AM	PM	PM	AM	AM		Leave Arrive		AM	PM	PM	AM	PM
6 45	8 15	1 00	9 45	3 30	......	....WAUKEGAN..	73.08	7 45	4 00	7 45	12 30	12 15
						3.60						
6 55	8 30	1 10	10 00	3 45	3.60	.NORTH CHICAGO.	69.48	7 20	3 40	7 25	12 10	11 50
						2.39						
7 00	8 35	1 15	10 05	3 50	5.99	......UPTON.......	67.09	7 15	3 35	7 20	12 05	11 40
						1.52						
7 05 / 7 20 3	8 45	2 00	10 15	4 00	7.51	.RONDOUT....	65.57	7 10 18	3 30	7 15	12 01	11 35
						5.30						
7 40	9 00	2 15	10 30	4 15	12.81	....LEITHTON.....	60.27	6 40	3 10	6 55	11 40	11 10
						7.05						
8 05	9 20	2 35	10 50 17	4 35	19.86	. LAKE ZURICH...	53.22	6 25	2 55	6 40	11 25	10 50
						3.91						
8 30	9 30	2 45 5	11 00	4 45	23.77	...BARRINGTON...	49.31	6 15	2 45 10	6 30	11 15	10 25
						5.48						
8 45	9 45	3 00	11 15	5 00	29.25	......SUTTON.....	43.83	6 00	2 30	6 15	11 00	10 00
						6.20						
9 00	10 00	3 15	11 30	5 15	35.45	...SPAULDING ...	37.63	5 45	2 15	6 00	10 45	9 45
						2.18						
......	......	......	......	......	37.63	...MUNGER ...	35.45	......	......	......	......	......
						1.90						
9 10	10 10	3 25	11 40	5 25	39.53	......WAYNE.....	33.55	5 30	2 00	5 45	10 30	9 15
						2.77						
......	......	......	......	......	42.30	...INGALTON.....	30.78	......	......	......	......	......
						1.49						
9 45	10 25	3 35	11 50	5 35	43.79	..WEST CHICAGO.	29.29	5 20	1 50	5 35	10 20	9 00
						7.10						
10 10	10 40	3 50	12 05	5 50	50.89	......EOLA.......	22.19	5 05	1 35	5 20	10 05	8 25
						1.56						
10 15	10 45	3 55	12 10	5 55	52.45	...EAST SIDING..	20.63	5 00	1 30	5 15	10 00	8 10
						1.71						
10 25	10 50	4 00	12 15	6 00	54.16	...FRONTENAC....	18.92	4 55	1 25	5 10	9 55	8 05
						5.99						
10 40	11 00	4 10	12 25	6 10	60.15	...NORMANTOWN..	12.93	4 40	1 10	4 55	9 40	7 50
						3.03						
10 50	11 05	4 15	12 30	6 15	63.18	.....WALKER......	9.90	4 30	1 00	4 45	9 30	7 35
						.48						
......	......	......	......	......	63.66	...PLAINFIELD...	9.42	......	......	......	......	......
						.74						
......	......	......	......	......	64.40	...GRAVEL PIT....	8.68	......	......	......	......	......
						2.66						
11 00	11 15	4 25	12 40	6 25	67.06	.COYNES......	6.02	4 20	12 50	4 35	9 20	7 25
						2.56						
......	......	......	......	......	69.62	.ROCKDALE JCT...	3.46	......	......	......	......	......
						1.09						
11 10	11 25	4 35	12 50	6 35	70.71	..BRIDGE JCT...	2.37	4 10	12 40	4 25	9 10	7 15
						2.37						
11 30	11 45	5 00	1 15	7 00	73.08	...EAST JOLIET...	....	4 00	12 30	4 15	9 00	7 05
AM	PM	PM	PM	AM		Arrive Leave		AM	PM	PM	PM	AM
18 Daily Ex. Sun.	**12** Daily	**10** Daily	**6** Daily	**4** Daily				**3** Daily	**5** Daily	**9** Daily	**11** Daily	**17** Daily Ex. Sun.

Double track extends from No. 1 crossover at East Joliet to a point 1861 feet east of MP J-37 on the Porter Branch and from Griffith to No. 1 crossover at Cavanaugh on the Joliet Division; also from No. 1 crossover Cavanaugh to Kirk Yard Jct. on the Gary Division.

Eastward trains will obtain Clearance Form A and train orders at Rock Island tower.

Engines may move with the current of traffic between Hartsdale and Griffith (either direction) without a clearance Form A.

Westward trains enroute to the Joliet Division will obtain Clearance Form A and train orders at Kirk Yard Junction, except as hereinafter provided. When a "Proceed, No orders" (green) indication is displayed on the train order signal it will be the authority for a regular train to use its schedule and the authority for any train other than a regular train or work train to proceed as an extra train to the destination for which the crew is called except crews on extra trains destined East of Griffith on the Porter Branch, it will be their authority to proceed as an extra train to Griffith. Crews called for turn around service out of Kirk Yard must obtain authority for their Eastward movement.

Rules D-97 and 97 of the Operating Department are hereby modified to the extent provided herein.

Between Cavanaugh and Kirk Yard is designated as the Kirk Yard Line (Gary Division); between Griffith and Porter is designated as the Porter Branch.

*TO-APPLIES: At Griffith to eastward trains; also to westward trains originating.

EASTERN SUBDIVISION—BETWEEN EAST JOLIET AND KIRK YARD

THIRD CLASS	SECOND CLASS			Distance From East Joliet	TIME TABLE No. 1 MAY 1, 1965	Distance From Kirk Yard	SECOND CLASS			THIRD CLASS
42	**44**	**6**	**4**				**9**	**43**	**11**	**41**
Loc. Frt.	Freight	Freight	Freight				Freight	Freight	Freight	Loc. Frt.
Daily	Daily	Daily	Daily		STATIONS		Daily	Daily	Daily	Daily
AM	PM	PM	AM		Leave Arrive		AM	AM	PM	PM
8 05	9 00	6 00	11 00	.....	....EAST JOLIET....	46.53	4 15	10 15	1 35	11 10
				2.65	..MARBLE FALLS..	43.88				
8 25	9 20	6 20	11 20	8.22	.....BRISBANE..... 5.57	38.31	3 50	9 50	1 10	10 45
8 45	9 40	6 40	11 40	14.04	...FRANKFORT.... 5.82	32.49	3 35	9 35	12 55	10 30
					—7.56—					
9 00	9 55	6 55	11 55	21.60	.....MATTESON..... 3.30	24.93	3 15	9 20	12 40	10 15
9 10	10 05	7 05	12 05	24.90	CHICAGO HEIGHTS 6.39	21.63	3 05	9 10	12 30	10 05
9 25	10 20	7 20	12 20	31.29	........DYER........ 2.52	15.24	2 50	8 55	12 15	9 50
9 35	10 30	7 30	12 30	33.81	...HARTSDALE.... 2.39	12.72	2 40	8 45	12 05	9 40
9 45	10 40	7 40	12 40	36.20	.....GRIFFITH..... —3.55—	10.33	2 30	8 35	11 55	9 30
				39.75	....VAN LOON.... 2.00	6.78				
				41.75	.....IVANHOE..... 1.11	4.78				
10 00	10 55			42.86	...CAVANAUGH.... 3.67	3.67		8 15		9 10
10 15	11 15			46.53	...KIRK YARD...	.....		8 05		9 00
AM	PM	PM	PM		Arrive Leave		AM	AM	AM	PM
42	**44**	**6**	**4**				**9**	**43**	**11**	**41**
Daily	Daily	Daily	Daily				Daily	Daily	Daily	Daily

PORTER BRANCH BETWEEN GRIFFITH AND PORTER

Railroad Connections	Train Order and Telephone Stations	Station Numbers	Capacity of Station Tracks	Capacity of Sidings	EASTWARD SECOND CLASS		Distance From East Joliet	TIME TABLE No. 1 MAY 1, 1965	Distance From Porter	WESTWARD SECOND CLASS	
					6	**4**				**9**	**11**
					Freight	Freight				Freight	Freight
					Daily	Daily		STATIONS		Daily	Daily
				Eastward 218 Westward 235	PM	PM		Leave Arrive		AM	AM
Erie-C&O-GT	C TO*	37	Yard		7 40	12 40	36.20	.....GRIFFITH..... —9.51—	20.50	2 30	11 55
NKP-PRR...	C TO	38	149	West 72 East 76	8 30	1 30	45.71	.....HOBART..... 6.39	10.99	2 00	11 20
B&O.......	....	39	72	20	8 55	1 55	52.10	.....McCOOL...... 1.37	4.60	1 20	10 20
Wabash.....	C TO	40	56	....	9 10	2 10	53.47	....CROCKER..... 3.23	3.23	1 10	10 10
NYC-C&O...	D TO	41	Yard	....	9 30	2 30	56.70	.....PORTER......	.....	1 00	10 00
					PM	PM		Arrive Leave		AM	AM
					6	**4**				**9**	**11**
					Daily	Daily				Daily	Daily

1976

JOLIET DIVISION – WESTERN SUBDIVISION – BETWEEN EAST JOLIET AND WAUKEGAN											
EASTWARD		Distance From Waukegan	**TIME-TABLE** No. 1 August 1, 1976	Distance From East Joliet	**WESTWARD**		Railroad Connections	Train Order and Telephone Stations	Station Numbers	Capacity of Sidings
SECOND CLASS					SECOND CLASS					
10 Loc. Frt.	**6** Freight				**5** Freight	**9** Loc. Frt.				
Daily Ex. Sun.	Daily		STATIONS		Daily	Daily Ex. Sat.				
PM	AM		Leave Arrive		PM	PM				
3 00	8 15	....	WAUKEGAN	73.08	7 00	9 00	C&NW	D TO	1	....
		3.60								
3 20	8 35	3.60	NORTH CHICAGO	69.48	6 40	8 40	....	....	1½	32
		2.39								
3 25	8 40	5.99	UPTON	67.09	6 35	8 35	C&NW	....	1A	
		1.52								Westward 120
3 30	8 45	7.51	ROUNDOUT	65.57	6 30	8 30	CMStP&P	C TO	2	
		5.30								
4 00	9 05	12.81	LEITHTON	60.27	6 10	8 00	Soo Line	D TO	3	73
		7.05								
4 30	9 20	19.86	LAKE ZURICH	53.22	5 55	7 30	....	D TO	5	65
		3.91								
4 45	9 30	23.77	BARRINGTON	49.31	5 45	7 15	C&NW	C TO	6	69
		5.48								
5 05	9 45	29.25	SUTTON	43.83	5 30	6 55	....	....	7	67
		6.20								
5 30	10 00	35.45	SPAULDING	37.63	5 15	6 40	CMStP&P	C TO	8	Westward 113
		2.18								
....	....	37.63	MUNGER	35.45	....	....	ICG	....	9	....
		4.67								
....	....	42.30	INGALTON	30.78	....	....	....	....	10	....
		1.49								
6 00	10 25	43.79	WEST CHICAGO	' 29.29	4 50	6 10	C&NW	C TO	11	....
		7.10								
6 20	10 40	50.89	EOLA	22.19	4 35	5 50	BN	....	13	85
		1.56								
6 35	10 45	52.45	EAST SIDING	20.63	4 30	5 35	BN	....	13	35
		1.71								
6 40	10 50	54.16	FRONTENAC	18.92	4 25	5 30	....	....	13A	105
		5.99								
6 55	11 05	60.15	NORMANTOWN	12.93	4 10	5 15	....	....	14	Westward ⎧
		3.03								
7 05	11 15	63.18	WALKER	9.90	4 00	5 00	....	....	15	250 ⎨
		.48								⎩
....	....	63.66	PLAINFIELD	9.42	....	....	....	D	27	....
		.74								
....	....	64.40	GRAVEL PIT	8.68	....	....	....		27A	
		2.66								
7 15	11 25	67.06	COYNES	6.02	3 50	4 50	....	....	28	....
		2.56								
....	....	69.62	ROCKDALE JCT.	3.46	....	....	....	....	29	....
		1.09								
7 25	11 35	70.71	BRIDGE JCT.	2.37	3 40	4 40	....	C TO	29A	....
		2.37								
7 40	11 45	73.08	EAST JOLIET	....	3 30	4 30	ICG AT&SF CRI&P CMStP&P	....	30	....
PM	AM		Arrive Leave		PM	PM				
10	**6**				**5**	**9**	Note: Capacity of sidings based on 55 foot cars.			
Daily Ex. Sun.	Daily				Daily	Daily Ex. Sat.				

JOLIET DIVISION – EASTERN SUBDIVISION – BETWEEN EAST JOLIET AND KIRK YARD

EASTWARD SECOND CLASS 42 Loc. Frt. Daily	Distance From East Joliet	TIME-TABLE No. 1 August 1, 1976 STATIONS	Distance From Kirk Yard	WESTWARD SECOND CLASS 41 Loc. Frt. Daily	Railroad Connections	Train Order and Telephone Stations	Station Numbers	Capacity of Sidings
AM		Leave Arrive		**AM**				
8 05	......	... EAST JOLIET ...	46.53	6 00	ICG AT&SF- CRI&P CMSt.P&P	C TO	30	....
	2.65	2.65 .. MARBLE FALLS ..	43.88	......		....	30A	....
	8.22	5.57 ..... BRISBANE	38.31	......	N&W	....	31	....
	14.04	5.82 ... FRANKFORT ...	32.49	......		....	32	....
	21.60	7.56 .... MATTESON	24.93	......	ICG	D TO	33	68
	24.90	3.30 CHICAGO HEIGHTS	21.63	......	C&EI-CHTT CMSt.P&P L&N	C TO	34	54
	31.29	6.39 .... DYER	15.24	......	L&N	C TO	35	73
	33.81	2.52 ... HARTSDALE ...	12.72	......	CR	C TO	36	Eastward 175
	36.20	2.39 ..... GRIFFITH	10.33	......	C&O-GT	C TO*	37	Westward 190
	39.75	3.55 .... VAN LOON	6.78	......	N&W	C TO*	61	....
	41.75	2.00 ..... IVANHOE	4.78	......		C	62	....
	42.86	1.11 ... CAVANAUGH ...	3.67	......			63	....
3 10	46.53	3.67 .... KIRK YARD	......	1 00		C TO	143	....
PM		Arrive Leave		**AM**				
42				**41**				
Daily				Daily				

NOTE: Capacity of sidings based on 55 ft. cars.

*TO-Applies: At Griffith to eastward trains and originating westward trains. At Van Loon to westward trains and originating eastward trains.

(D-97-97) Eastward trains will obtain Clearance Form A and/or Train Orders at Rock Island Tower. Crews called for turnaround service out of East Joliet must obtain authority for their westward movement.

Westward trains enroute to the Joliet Division via Lake Front Line and/or Kirk Yard Line will obtain Clearance Form A and Train Orders at Kirk Yard Junction except as hereinafter provided. When a "Proceed, No Orders" (green) indication is displayed on the train order signal, it will be the authority for a regular train or work train to proceed as an extra train to the destination for which the crew is called except crews on extra trains destined East of Griffith on the Porter Line, it will be their authority to proceed as an extra train to Griffith.

Crews called for turnaround service out of Kirk Yard must obtain authority for their eastward movement.

C.L.S.&E. WYE - A proceed indication displayed on a governing signal will be the authority for trains from the Lake Front Line enroute to the Joliet Division via C.L.S.&E. Wye to proceed as an extra train to the destination for which the crew is called except crews on extra trains destined east of Griffith on the Porter Line, it will be their authority to proceed as an extra train to Griffith. Crews called for turnaround service must obtain authority for their eastward movement on the Joliet Division.

Engines may move with the current of traffic between Hartsdale and Griffith (either direction) without a Clearance Form A.

Rules D-97 and 97 of the Operating Department are modified to conform with the above.

Double track extends from No. 1 crossover at East Joliet to No. 1 crossover at Cavanaugh on the Joliet Division; and from No. 1 crossover Cavanaugh to Kirk Yard Junction on the Gary Division.

One of the EJ&E's big Mikados, the mainstays of heavy freight service in the steam era, was no. 765, photographed at Gary in July of 1932. As with a number of examples of EJ&E heavy steam power, this locomotive later went to the DM&IR as their no. 1330 and was subsequently on display at Gary. *(Harold K. Vollrath collection)*

In the diesel era, there was no EJ&E locomotive which equalled the distinctive image of the Baldwin center cabs. This perfectly lit view shows rebuilt No. 909 at Waukegan on October 1, 1966. *(Arnold Menke collection)*

RESOURCES

Auffart, A.M., *The Elgin, Joliet and Eastern Railway Company: A History of the Early Development of a Regional Railroad*, EJ&E, Chicago, 1988.

Divisional time tables, various years, EJ&E.

Equipment and motive power rosters, various years, EJ&E.

Interviews with EJ&E staff personnel listed in Acknowledgements.

Jaenicke, Paul W., and Ralph A. Eisenbrandt, *Elgin, Joliet and Eastern Railway* (Images of Rail series), Arcadia Publishing, Chicago, 2007.

J-Milepost (employee magazine), various years, EJ&E.

Mechanical records and diagrams, various years, EJ&E.

Official Railway Equipment Register, The Railway Equipment and Publication Co., New York, various years.

A few other sources are cited in the text.

This original watercolor painting by railroad artist Ernie Towler shows one of the Baldwin center cabs in an unusually rural setting for the EJ&E.

INDEX

For a final look at the EJ&E, here's a view from atop the grain elevator in Plainfield, Illinois, near Walker and the junction with the Coal City Branch. Center cabs 914 and 915 power a westward freight heavy with gondolas of steel products, a quintessential EJ&E cargo.

(EJ&E photo, probably by Richard Benson; Richard Buike collection)

The text of this book is set in Bembo, an elegant face derived from a type designed by Francesco Griffo for Aldus Manutius of Venice in 1495 for the book *De Ætna* by Pietro Bembo (later Cardinal Bembo). As part of a series of revivals, this typeface was recut in 1929 for the Lanston Monotype Corporation of England, under the direction of Stanley Morison, and named in honor of Cardinal Bembo.

In early printing, Roman and italic faces were not used together, so Griffo did not design an italic to go with his Roman. The italic face Morison chose to accompany Griffo's Roman is one designed by Giovantonio Tagliente in 1524. The digital version of Bembo used here was created in 1990 and is from Monotype.

The titling face is Hamilton, named for William Hamilton Page (1829–1906), a self-taught designer of wood types who patented this spirited face in 1887. Several weights were subsequently added to the original. It was digitized by font designer Tom Rickner for Font Bureau in 1993. Many original Hamilton wood types are preserved at the Hamilton Wood Type & Printing Museum in Two Rivers, Wisconsin.